Table of Contents

Chapter One – The Shelter

Before I knew I needed them, I had my doubts about people being prescribed medication for mental illness and whether or not it was necessary. After these next 10 days, my doubts no longer existed.

I was walking up a city street that would eventually take me somewhere downtown Red Deer, Alberta. I had my little bag of groceries, with my bottle of orange juice, and some fruit in one hand, my violin in the other. I wanted to feel somewhat invisible so I put up the hoodie of my red Detroit Pistons sweatshirt and headed towards the complete unknown. As I walked further, I saw a group of men hanging out having a cigarette with each other on the other side. There were four of them, all native men who looked a little rough around the edges. Two were sitting down on the concrete steps, and two were standing up. I was walking with my head down and turned just slightly so I could glance in their direction. When they saw me approaching on the other side, one of the men tapped the shoulder of the guy beside him and gestured for him to look over my way. Their conversation ran silent for a moment. Then I heard one of the men say in a deep and mocking tone, "Now there's an example of a spoiled rich kid."

I was really taken aback by this comment. I couldn't believe the misperception of my life. Whichever one of them said it must have said it loud enough for me to hear. It could have been whispered silently amongst them, but it wasn't. They were telling me what they thought simply judging by my walking by.

I had made my way anyway I could to make ends meet in this world. I was far from a spoiled rich kid, and I was going to let these native men know how wrongly they had judged me. I was feeling homeless while the native men thought I looked privileged, all because I was carrying a violin. My father is a hard working bricklayer. My mother was a secretary until she had my two younger brothers. She then became a stay at home mom. We were taught to work hard for everything we have. I have had a job ever since I was 16 years old, and I babysat before that. I had never once asked my parents for money.

I walked up to the next set of lights and waited until the green light shone in the direction across the street where I was headed. This action that I was about to take was completely out of character for me. Had I had a good night's rest, I seriously doubt I would have been heading back towards a group of gruff native guys that had just called me out. I would probably have just shaken my head to myself and quietly noted how wrong of a perception that was. But, that's not the case. My guards were down. I was feeling ballsy and slightly invincible, or overly confident that nothing really bad could come by me telling these guys they were wrong.

I walked up to them and before they even knew I was there I started to speak. "Excuse me, but I overheard what you said and I want you to know that you're totally wrong." The looks on their faces were stricken with shock. One man took a step back with his mouth agape and listened to me with his eyes wide open.

"I just quit a tree planting job that I was going to do all summer. And I haven't slept for three days."

The tune they had before with my passing by instantly melted away. I could see a new found respect for my courage and honesty in my approach to them.

"I'm waiting for my bus to leave tonight to take me to my sister's place. But I have all day to spare. So do you guys know anywhere I could go that someone like me might like to see while I'm here in Red Deer?"

One of the guys suggested I go sleep in a park for a few hours. But I let him know that I've already tried to sleep and it's pointless for me right now.

So he asked me what I needed, a hot shower, a cup of coffee? That was exactly what I needed. I needed to be refreshed. He said I could get all that just down the stairs. As it turned out, these guys were hanging out in front of a Native Run homeless shelter. I wasn't too proud to go down those stairs. One of the men sitting on the steps asked me if I could play the violin I was carrying. I told him I just picked it up this week, but I've been playing the guitar for about 7 years now and I've always wanted to learn the violin.

He asked me if he could see it. I looked him in the eyes and asked him if I could trust him with it while I went inside to shower. I doubt these guys were used to complete strangers trusting them with their prized possessions. He had a glow in his eyes when he looked at me and nodded his head yes. I gave it to him, said "thank you", and turned to go inside the building.

I walked down the long set of stairs and turned left to go through the doorway at the bottom. The area was open. There were tables and chairs set up with about 25 people sitting around in them, mostly native and all men or teenaged boys. They were sitting around either singularly or in their own groups. There was a TV on at the back of the room, but everyone's eyes were on me as I stood in the door-way.

I walked past the tables at the front that had coffee and snacks lying out and went directly to the volunteer counter and asked about having a shower. The man behind the counter was very warm towards me. He gave me a towel and a little bottle of shampoo and showed me the entrance-way to the shower room around the right-hand side of the counter.

The shower room was bright, tiled white and well lit. There were two sinks directly ahead of me and I walked towards them. I looked at myself in the mirror. I told myself not to be scared, that it was okay to shower here. It was empty except for me, which I was grateful for. I hoped no one else would come in while I was showering. I looked at the two stalls that were available and chose one to use. They had privacy doors on them and a place to take your clothes off before stepping into the shower. I went in and locked the metal door behind me.

I read the print out that was hanging on the back of the door telling all who use this shower to clean up after themselves. It did seem pretty clean. I put my bag of groceries on the wooden chair in the corner of the stall and started to take my clothes off. My actions were slow, my exhaustion of not having slept for three days was lingering over me, but I was careful to not let any of my clothes touch the floor. Every piece made it to the chair.

I pushed the nozzle head down so the water wouldn't blast on me when I turned it on. Once the temperature felt nice and hot I moved the nozzle back up and stepped into the blazing stream.

"Ahhhhhhhhh."

My eyes were closed, my head down, my hands on the tiled shower wall before me, and the water was pelting my head and running down all over my naked body. I had never felt so good. This was a medicinal shower.

Time stood still, luxuriously and heavenly still. I turned around and put my head back and gently rubbed my face with the water, breathing in the peace and calm of washing away my sleepless filth. The water flowed and flowed and showered me with its freshness. It was the longest shower of my life. I ran the water cold and still I stayed standing beneath it.

When I was finally finished, I turned the water off, stepped out of the open concept shower stall and towelled myself off. My energy was still low, I needed to take a moment and sit down on the chair where I had hung my belongings. For a moment I just sat there, still naked and rested my head in my hands. I knew I needed to get dressed and get out of the shower, but I just needed to take a moment; a quiet, still moment.

I got dressed, in the same clothes I had just taken off. The only clothes I had on me at the time. As I was leaving the shower room I took one last look in the mirror, adjusted my damp hair and prepared to face what lay on the other side of the shower room wall.

"Where do I put my towel?" I asked the man behind the counter who had given it to me earlier.

"Just right there in that basket," was his kind reply while pointing to the corner behind me.

"Oh, k, thanks," I smiled at him.

I put the towel in the basket and looked around, in search of the coffee I was told would be down here. Around the counter I walked to the table of refreshments. There was the coffee pot waiting to fill my cup. The Styrofoam cups were right beside it, so I grabbed one and started to fill it with the black liquid I was yearning for.

"Oh, a girl, now we're going to have to watch what we say," was the voice I heard behind me, an angry and jaded voice.

I turned around to find four boys sitting at a square table kitty corner to me.

"You can say whatever you want," I retorted back, with a little more fever than I had expected to come out of my mouth.

"She's feisty," was the reply to the group, as the boy that said it got up from the table and went out the doorway and up the stairs that headed back outside.

I felt confidence come over me. I wasn't going to let anyone intimidate me while I was here, and in return I could feel a growing respect for my outward projection.

I was starting to worry about my violin. So I took my coffee and went back outside to get it from the men I left it with. Once I got up the stairs and out the door all I saw was the empty steps where the men were sitting earlier. A little dose of panic came over me. Where were they? Where was my violin? I turned to go back inside the doorway, but there was a large native man standing in front of it, blocking me from going in.

"How much is that violin worth to you?" He asked.

I was a little shocked and took a step back from the door. He had his foot resting in the doorway, the door leaning slightly open upon it. His disheveled appearance became apparent to me and I knew I was talking to someone who had seen the darker side of life first hand. His black eyes peered into mine and he asked me again.

"How much is it worth to you?"

"I don't know, it's not for sale," I fumbled out nervously, but trying to keep my cool.

"Priceless, eh?" He was still blocking the door on me. I wanted to get back inside, so I grabbed the handle and pulled.

"Is it worth that cup of coffee, remember to give back, eh. Here, let me have a sip of it."

I handed him my coffee with a little disgust and said, "Keep it," thinking to always remember to watch my drink in case someone tried to slip something in it, then went through the door and back down the stairs.

I walked in the room and asked loudly so everyone could hear, "Has anyone seen my violin?"

An older native man, probably somewhere in his 40's or 50's, looked at me and pointed over to my right at a table that was pushed up against the wall. There rested my black violin case, handle up. A feeling of delight and reassurance lit through me. I walked over to the table, picked it up and went to sit down near the man that pointed it out to me.

"Can you play that thing?" He asked.

"Well, do you like the sound of cat scratches?" I beamed back at him with an enormous smile.

He looked at me with a quizzical smirk pasted on his face and replied. "Sure, whatever you can play."

I set the case on my table and opened it up, revealing a 19th century red mahogany violin. Releasing the bow from its sitting place I tightened its strings to a pressure I thought I could play with and stroked some rosin over them. I then took hold of the neck of the violin and placed it over the collar bone on my left shoulder.

I took to playing it seriously. My concentration set in and all I was thinking about was the sound that this beautiful piece of crafted wood and strings could make. I started on the high string and soothingly stroked it with my taught bow. Gazing only at the strings of my violin I began to quicken my pace and soothe over the string beside it, bouncing back and forth between the two, adding a third and fourth string to the rapturing melancholic sound I was producing, deeper rich tones intermingled with the lighter uplifted whines. Bouncing back and forth on those four strings overcame my entire existence, and listening to it filled me with joy. Then I brought the bow to its final bounce, and lifted it from the strings.

At the end of my brief performance the man asked, "Is that your first song?"

I was flattered by his comment, and humble in my response. "I don't know, I was just playing around. "

He seemed like a serious kind of man. He looked at me thoughtfully.

"Well, now, you could be a busker. You could make some money that way."

The idea thrilled me and scared me at the same time. I took it as a great compliment. Maybe I do have musical talent. Maybe other people can see that I am a musician. There have been moments in my life where I wanted to be so care-free that I would allow myself to throw caution to the wind and try to make ends meet purely on the love for music and the artistry that lies within my heart and soul, but to live on the streets as a busker? That was beyond my comfort level. That was only something of a daydream, a wonder of a life, not reality. Now, this man was telling me that I could do it. I let myself get carried away with the thought for a moment, but the wayward lifestyle was too much for me to fathom. It scared me to think those thoughts because I felt on the verge of insanity when I did.

Chapter Two – Meeting Allan

When I put the violin back in its case I took it back over to the table where I had gotten it from and walked over to make myself another cup of coffee, seeing as the scary guy outside took mine.

"Nice boots, I can tell you're a workin' girl." There was a white man standing beside me with a cup of coffee in his hand. He was very jittery, and seemed to not have complete control over his body movements. His arms twitched rambunctiously and he couldn't stay still. But he had kind blue eyes. He looked to be in his fifties with his hair mostly grey, but the darkness of its colour was still apparent.

He was referring to the work boots my friend Diamond had given to me while I was at her cabin just a couple of days ago. They were brand new CSA approved steel toed leather boots with a raised heel. I loved them because of the colour of the leather, purple with light tan patched on the heel and toe.

"Thanks, my friend just gave them to me not long ago," was my reply.

"Are you lookin' for work, cause I know of some stuff around. I got a roofin job lined up through this company that pays cash. Do you want in on something like that?" He seemed harmless enough to me, and I kind of felt bad that he had such little control over his body movements. I didn't know what could have caused it, or what was wrong with him.

"Oh, no, that's okay. I'm not lookin' for work, I'm just waitin' on my bus. I'm only here in Red Deer for the day."

"What's yer name, sweetheart?" He asked.

"Erin, what's yours?"

"I'm Allan," he put out his hand for me and had a smile on his pale face. I took his hand and shook it firmly.

"You smoke, Erin?"

"Sometimes, I can sure use one now."

"Well come on outside to my van, we'll have a smoke."

I followed him out of the shelter, carrying my bag of groceries and my cup of coffee, minus my violin. He opened the door for me at the top of the stairs and smiled as I walked past him and through the doorway. He went to cross the street and I trailed behind him a couple of steps, making sure it was safe to cross. On the other side he stood next to a blue van by the passenger side door. I looked around and saw three native men sitting on a public bench on the sidewalk not too far away. Allan gave me a smoke and lit it for me, then proceeded to light his own. I took a drag, and blew the smoke out.

"You alright, little girl? You look lost." I felt dazed, and in a dream, but not lost. I figured it was probably the fact that I hadn't slept in three days.

"I do?"

"Yeah, I can see it in your eyes." He was standing kind of close to me and staring at me pretty intensely, but he didn't scare me.

"Come on," he said, as he opened up the passenger side door of the mini-van. "Have a seat in my van."

I got in, put my bag on the floor by my feet and took another drag of my cigarette. He walked around the back of the van and got in the driver's side.

Leaning forward towards the steering wheel Allan reached into his coat pockets to take out his pack of smokes. The ashtray in his van was full. The dashboard could use a nice wipe down with Armor-All, the carpet needed vacuumed. He put the pack of smokes on the dash.

"They call me Big Blue," he said, as he reached under his seat and pulled out one of the biggest blue dildos I had ever seen. He had a huge grin on his face as he held the dildo placed on the seat in between his legs. I couldn't believe my eyes.

I just kind of laughed and said, "Yeah, that nickname also matches your blue eyes." He put the dildo back under the seat.

He started saying something about women. How it's hard to meet a nice girl.

"I had this lady in my van the other day. She wound up pukin' all over by the end of the night."

She must have been really drunk, I thought to myself as I looked at Allan and could see the hardness of his life from the choices he had made in the past.

Reaching out to put his hand on my knee while he talked I became a little uncomfortable. He didn't leave it there long; he just patted it and carried on with his hand motions as he spoke. He was very light and pleasant with his body language at this time. It seemed like the twitching had passed.

"I can tell you're a nice girl. You're sweet."

"Listen," I said, "I'm just going to be up-front and frank with you. If you think there is a chance between you and me and that's why you're talking to me, then I want you to know you're wrong. There's no way I'm having sex with you." I was firm, and straight forward, and not messing around.

"What?" He looked at me a bit quizzically. "What made you say that?"

"I just want to be straight up with you and let you know where I'm coming from. Besides, I'm seeing someone back home."

I have always thought honesty is the best policy, and I didn't want to give Allan the wrong idea. At times I find it easier to be this straight forward with perfect strangers, especially if you know you're never going to see them again.

"What's his name?" he asked.

"Well, actually, it's a girl. Her name is Sarah." No point in lying to him.

"Oh, really, so you're gay." He pointed out what to me was obvious.

"Yeah, I am" simply put.

He didn't seem to be bothered by this statement. He just drew another drag from his cigarette while nodding his head.

"You know, it's like some girls have this chip on their shoulder towards guys; like they resent their attention." It was obvious to me that he was talking from his own personal experience.

"Well, I don't, I like guys. It's fun hanging out with them, they have better times than girls it seems, they're more fun to talk to. I just wish it could be like it was in kindergarten, when guys and girls could be friends without the complication of sexuality."

He was thoughtful for a few seconds before he said, "Hmm, so you're not lookin for a job, eh?"

I liked Allan; he was easy to be around.

"Nah, it's tempting, but I gotta get to my sister's place. Like I said, my bus leaves tonight. And I have to get my bags out of the bus terminal before it closes." There was a part of me that wondered about what it would be like to stay in Red Deer for a while, if a job was going to fall that easily into my lap. But, clearly I wasn't thinking straight. I didn't realize I had too many ideas running around in my head already.

"What time does it close?" He asked.

"By four o'clock."

"What time's yer bus at?"

"It leaves at 9 o'clock, so I guess I'll have to wait around with my bags outside the terminal for like 5 hours."

"Tell you what, we can go pick up your bags, you can leave 'em in my van 'til yer bus leaves." He seemed very sincere in his offer, like it would be no trouble at all and he'd like to help me out.

"Really? That would help a lot, are you sure?" I asked.

"Yeah, no problem, let's go get 'em." He smiled again, found his keys and started the van.

Chapter Three – The Ride

Red Deer is a fair sized city and the streets were pretty busy with other motor vehicles. Allan seemed to know his way around though. We weren't very far from the bus terminal, it probably only took us about 5 minutes to get there. When he pulled in he slowed the vehicle down and came to a stop in front of the doors I had to go in. Neither one of us was in a big hurry. Allan seemed to always have a mouthful of thoughts, sometimes mumbles running through him. I got the impression that he hadn't really talked to anyone for quite some time, not someone who was really listening to him anyway.

While we were sitting there in his van he picked his pack of smokes up off the dash and opened it. He had some half smokes in there, and I suddenly realized just how poor Allan was. He still offered me another one.

"Are you sure you can afford to give me a smoke?" I sincerely asked. I didn't want to take something that might be more important to him than it was to me.

He looked at me truly surprised by my thoughtful nature. It was like he couldn't believe that I would even think to say something like that.

"Yeah, sure, go on," he insisted. So I had another cigarette, and so did he.

"Here," I said, as I reached into my bag of groceries I was carrying around. "Have a drink." I passed him my bottle of unopened orange juice.

"This is a new bottle," He said.

"Yeah, I got it at the grocery store this morning."

He looked at me quizzically. "No, it's yours."

"Go on, take it." I made him take it. He looked like he could use a drink other than the free coffee they were giving out at the shelter.

He opened up the bottle and drank half of it in a couple of gulps. When he tried to offer me some, I wouldn't take it back. It was his now, and I wasn't about to share a bottle with him.

His jittery movements came back as he was trying to talk to me. His shoulders would thrust inward on him and he'd move forwards and backwards as he spoke. I tried to make out what he was saying in between mumbles of sounds.

"…I saw my brother get shot right in front of me. My family isn't good for me. I need to just break away from them and start over." He opened up to me about the darkest parts of his life and psyche.

"Wow, that's pretty rough, I can't imagine that." I hauled on my smoke while I listened to him. He was still jerking back and forth.

"I've hit rock bottom, I'm sleeping in my van, I'm trying to get by from job to job." He was being very sincere. He was purging his true thoughts and feelings out for my ears to listen to, and I thought it was a very special moment, and I owed it to him to listen and try to help him.

"What is it you want to do with your life?" I asked him.

He looked at me and answered, "I'm a truck driver, I want to drive truck again. I have my license for it."

"Well, why don't you try to do that then? There's gotta be truck driver jobs around here."

"Why am I telling you all this? I feel like I can really talk to you. God, I need to find a good woman."

Looking at him, in the state that he was in, barely sounding audible in his speech and twitching off and on throughout the little time that I had spent with him I had to ask, "Are you okay? Your body is twitching pretty bad."

"Yeah, yeah, I'm just not used to talking to someone like this so much. It's my nerves, I'm a nervous person."

"Well, you're going to have to overcome that, there's nothing to be nervous about." Something still seemed odd to me, but I couldn't quite put my finger on it.

Then he confessed, "I took some crack last night, and I'm still coming down from it."

"Holy shit, really? Well Allan, you look like shit. You're never going to find a good woman in the state you're in. Man, your body is twitchin' all over the place, it's like you're going through mini spasms or something. You've gotta get your shit together before you can even think of getting a nice girl."

"Reeeally?" He didn't even know he was doing it, or how bad of shape he was in. I mimicked his movements to him, flailed my body around like he had been and showed him what he looked like. He was embarrassed; I couldn't believe he didn't know.

"The only people I know around here want to stick needles in my arms." He told me.

"Well you gotta get away from that shit. Think about what it's doing to you." I felt like I was trying to save him from a life of destruction through sheer honesty. I finished my smoke and chucked the butt out the window, "I'm going to go get my bags."

"Ok," he said, and waited in the van. He'd probably heard more than enough for the time being.

When I came back out of the bus station with my two big duffel bags and my knapsack, Allan got out of the van and walked around to the other side to open up the sliding doors for me. He helped me put the bags inside. He still seemed really happy to be hanging out with me. I felt like we were both doing each other a favour, and God was with me.

"There now, all set." He said, after he had adjusted the last bag in place in the center of the van. He pulled the sliding door shut with a big toothy smile and seemed prouder than a peacock spreading its feathers as he walked around back to the other side of the van where he could get back in the driver's seat. I opened my passenger side door and got back in too.

He started up the van, backed up and started to drive. I just assumed we'd be heading back to the shelter.

Allan's driving was a little erratic, and I didn't always feel safe with him behind the wheel, but I decided to stay calm and believe that we'd get to our destination safely.

"I have some place I want to show you." He told me.

"Where?" I asked, not sure I wanted to travel all over with him.

"It's one of the nicest parks in town, right off the Red Deer River." He beamed at me.

"I don't know, Allan, maybe we should just go back to the shelter. "

"What, come on, we've got all day, lemme show you somethin' nice."

"No, Allan, I think we should just get back."

After I had said it, I thought to myself, why not? My day was turning out to be quite adventurous. Allan didn't scare me, why not have a tour of a place I had never been, and most likely would never be again.

"Oh, alright, let's go."

And with that, Allan cheerfully drove to his intended destination. He was telling me how it was close to the golf course and how I'm going to love it. I was watching the roads and buildings pass me by as we drove. I remember seeing Gaetz Avenue, and

HWY 2A coming up in some sort of roundabout, but that didn't mean much to me. I was a tourist. Allan was my guide. We were further away from downtown, that's really all I knew.

Allan exited off the busy highway and drove down and around a windy turn-off. I could see the park setting ahead of us. When Allan passed by the paved parking lot and kept driving along the park road, my senses peaked. We were headed towards a more woodsy area, leaving the open space and few people walking around behind us. I sat up more erect and looked intently out at my surroundings, which were all treed. I felt nervous.

"Where are you going?"

"I'm just taking you through the park,"

"I don't want to go here, let's go back to the start," I was starting to feel a little panicked.

"Hey, don't worry; I'm just lookin' for a good spot."

"No, I don't want to go this way, please, take me back to the beginning," I was full blown scared now and completely mad at myself for getting into this situation. I looked back at my bags sitting in the van and realized just how vulnerable I was for the first time.

"Easy now," Allan must have seen how scared I was getting. He drove around a little gravel cul-de sac.

"Please, take me back." I was almost pleading.

"Ok, ok" We were heading back. I felt relieved.

He parked the van at that first parking lot we had originally traveled past, facing the opened area. There was open grass ahead of us, a children's playground just off to the left, and paved walking trails throughout. Over to the right was the tree line. A handful of park goers were scattered about, couples walking together, some children playing on the climbers, parents watching them while chatting amongst themselves. I felt a lot safer here, and my panic quickly dissipated.

Once parked, Allan reached for his pack of cigarettes again. I declined, as he lit another one. He never seemed to be in much of a hurry to get out of his vehicle. We also never talked about how scared I had just gotten. It was like it never happened. I was the one in a hurry to get out, suddenly charged by the idea to go and check out a new park scene I had never been to before.

"Come on, lets' go," I said, as I opened up my door and jumped out.

Careless. That would be a good word to sum up my actions at this time. Completely careless. I mean, I had just had the fright of a lifetime, textbook fear, and moments later I'm just ready to carry on as if it never happened; like I was some kind of saint that God would protect through any situation, even if I threw myself at the wolves trying to make them into puppy dogs. Or, maybe Allen really was a puppy dog. Maybe he just lost his way and became very shaggy and unbrushed in his adult years. This is what I thought, anyway.

He got out of the truck and we started walking on the paved path. "Here, let's go in there," he was guiding me through the trees. There was a little opening where walkers had made their own path into the wooded area. I couldn't see where it was headed to. I hesitated, looked to the side and saw that the paved path just went around the park and didn't really go anywhere. I liked wooded paths, especially compared to open and paved walkways.

"Come on," he said again. And I followed him.

We were walking through a tiny patch of forest and bush. Sticks were crackling underneath my steps. Gusts of freshness filled the air. We hadn't gone very far when we came upon another path up ahead of us, heading in the opposite direction both left and right from us. Allan never hesitated; he obviously knew where we were going. We walked straight ahead, through tall grasses and down a little deer trail to hit water. It was the Red Deer River, and it was bold, wide, beautiful, and gushing with travel speed.

When I saw the river I was in awe of it. There really is nothing like being taken aback by a piece of nature. I sat down on the riverbank in a patch of open grass and looked out at it. The sound of the gushing water passing by is calming. The view of its natural force is inspiring.

Allan sat down a little behind me. He had his black go-cup of coffee in his hand. The sun was beaming on this clear, blue sky day, and Allan was full of stories.

"You should've seen me in my younger days. Boy, did I work hard. I could clear a whole acre of land by myself. That's how come I came out to Alberta. I had work logging. And I had a wife. She could stay in the cabin while I cut trees down all day. I loved it." I just listened. He was telling me about "the good 'ole days.

He was proud of himself, and what he had accomplished. When he was a younger man, he had lived out his dreams by moving to a richer province and making a good living by working hard. But somehow in the process he had lost his wife. He never really said what happened, but he did say they had parted. And by the slumping of his body as he said it, he never really got over her. He did say he had married a second time, but again, that marriage had failed. As well as the logging market, that failed him too after a time.

"The times hit Alberta hard," I can only assume he meant the recession in the 1980's. I didn't ask a lot of questions. I just felt like Allan needed to dump his story on somebody, and who better to tell than someone who seemed to care?

I couldn't help but to look out at the flowing water as he spoke. All that he said washed away up the river and carried on to another time.

I got out my phone and texted my girlfriend back home. I wanted her to know where I was, what I was doing, and who I was doing it with. There was a part of me that wanted to share this whole exhilarating experience with her. The other part of me did it for my own safety. I took a picture of Allan.

"Here, Allan, let me get a photo of you, I want to send it to Sarah!" No objections from Allan at all. He was glad to have his picture taken. He sat there with a very natural, full smile, his head tilted slightly to the left side of the frame. He looked good in his purple button up long sleeved shirt. The sunny day complimented his bright disposition. He was very content to be sitting here, talking with me now.

I sent the picture to Sarah, with a text that read:

ME: This is my new friend Allan!

She wrote back instantaneously.

Sarah: What? What's going on? Where are you?

I wasn't expecting her response. I was feeling so free-spirited and alive that I just thought she would share the experience with me, enjoy being entertained by a new story. But I could feel the frantic and concerned angst through the text.

ME: It's okay, trust me.

Sarah: Where are you!

ME: I'm hanging out with Allan down by the Red Deer River

Sarah: Who is Allan? You should be at the bus station, where you're safe.

ME: Trust me, I'm okay. I'm listening to my instincts. Allan's a good guy.

I went on to write Sarah a book of a text all about how I met Allan and that I'm okay and listening to my instincts. She was not impressed with me at all. She thought I should be staying at the bus station the whole 10 hours I had to wait for my bus to come. I couldn't do that. That would be way too boring for me to stare at some bus station wall waiting for time to pass when there are places to walk to and things to see that I haven't seen before. I never planned on meeting someone and hanging out, but I thought my time was passing by in an interesting fashion. It felt like a mini adventure for me. Sarah thought I was putting myself in danger, and in all honesty she was right. I was being very reckless and quite unsafe, but at the time I didn't see it like that. She was very angry with me and thought I was acting really strange. I thought she was really over-reacting and trying to make me be something I'm not.

Meanwhile, Allan was sitting next to me, still talking and wanting my attention. He wasn't twitching anymore, and although he didn't always have the easiest voice to understand, he wasn't mumbling as much either. He seemed so delighted, and the colour of his skin seemed to be changing before my eyes, going from a paler grey, to rosiness in his cheeks. I did not feel threatened by him at all. He was looking at me texting my friend. I told him I was texting my girlfriend and letting her know where I was, but I didn't tell him she was really upset about it.

My relationship with Sarah was a fire-filled one. Right from day one we fought a lot. But we also both really wanted it to work at the same time. There was an equal amount of good times as there were bad times. She was a very strict personality and I wasn't. She was a rule maker, I was a rule breaker. We both had strong values and morals and wanted and believed in the same things, but never seemed to be able to grow together. Our relationship was at a stand-still, yet neither one of us wanted to admit it at this time. Her profession was a jail guard, mine, well; I had been a professional searcher. I've had many jobs, as well as many hobbies, and hadn't figured it all out just yet. I just knew I didn't want to settle into a life that didn't feed my soul.

I left things with Sarah through text on not a very good note at that time. I was trying to convince her of something that she wasn't going to be convinced of. She did not think I was safe. I did.

After sitting with Allan at the river for half an hour or so, I felt like I had gotten a glimpse of his past. I thought he wound up in the present state his life is in now by not being able to handle the hardship he had encountered in his life; not being able to handle having lost his relationships, not being able to handle his family circumstances, and not being able to sustain a good working life because of it. Somewhere in Allan there was a lost soul, making bad decisions.

It was time for us to leave the river. We got up and I followed him back up the deer trail through the tall grasses. When we came out of the wooded area and back out onto the paved path, Allan reached for my hand and walked with me out into public like that. I noted mentally that it was an odd thing to do. And I admit my thought was that he was doing it to make appearances to the rest of the public eye that we were a couple. This could be construed as a sign that perhaps Allan did have some shady intentions, but I wasn't scared of it, and I didn't think anything bad would come of it. I didn't keep holding his hand. I don't know if I let go, or if he did, or if we both did, but we didn't hold hands for long. We were walking individually to his van the rest of the way. Maybe Allan has done this before. I'm sure Allan has done a lot of things in his life that I will never know about.

Chapter Four – The Supper

We drove back to the shelter. Allan parked in the same spot he was in before and when I told him I should go and get my violin. He agreed.

"There's a lot of thieves around, you know. You can't trust these people with your things." He told me. It felt like he was looking after me. I got the impression he cared. I got out, and jogged over to the shelter door; went down the stairs again, and into the open room.

I walked straight over to the table where I had left my violin and found it there safe and sound. When I turned to leave, a native lady stopped to talk to me. She was one of the helpers, or volunteers at the shelter. She was an older lady, probably in her early sixties.

"The shelter closes at four," she said. It was just before four. I had just made it on time to pick up my violin.

"Where are you going?" she asked me. When she spoke to me she looked me straight and intensely in my eyes. I got the feeling she was looking to see if I was high on something, or intoxicated somehow.

"I'm just hanging out with Allan," I said.

She must have known who Allan was; he must have frequented this place enough times. Still looking in my eyes, she told me of a soup kitchen held at the Seventh Day Adventist Church that was holding a free supper tonight at 5 o'clock. She thought Allan and I should go I guess. She gave me directions, and I remembered the key points. I told her thank you. I looked around at the rest of the people who were in the shelter and said goodbye to whoever was looking at me. I was happy, and I felt like they could see a light in my eyes.

I climbed the stairs, reunited with my violin, for the last time. When I opened the door a native man handed me a set of four little comic books. I took them, and thanked him. As it turns out, they were religious comic book stories trying to "save souls" by bringing them to Christianity. Published by Chick Publications out of California, they were titled "Allah Had No Son", "Somebody Goofed", "The Fool", and "Titanic." I took it as a sign. I believed I was a spiritual person going about religion and saving souls in my own way. I wasn't in danger, I was helping Allan.

I got back to his van and told him about the free supper.

"We should go!" I said. "She said to go up this street and take a left at that building over there at the first set of lights," I was pointing up the street to the right hand side out my window.

"Sure, okay, sounds good."

"I don't know about you, but I could use a good meal"

"Yeah, I'd like that!"

We were on the road again, on a mission to find the Seventh Day Adventist Church. I told Allan the directions exactly as I remembered them, but it turned out not to be as easy as it sounded. It's a good thing we had an hour to find the place. We went around in circles for a while; I obviously missed something in the direction giving.

Allan's body was acting up on him again as he was driving. He was going the speed limit, but he always seemed distracted and talked incessantly while he drove. He wasn't a very focused person. He definitely needed to figure out how to control his mind and gather his thoughts. That's what made driving with him a little scary. I know he mentioned wanting to be a truck driver and he wasn't erratic in the way that he wasn't driving safely, but he didn't seem to have the mind power to focus himself very well. His attention span wasn't very good, I also questioned his memory. I assumed it was the drug-use that could have caused this.

I felt calm, being lost didn't bother me. It didn't seem to bother Allan either. He just seemed happy to be on a mission to find it, like it was a challenge for him.

At one point he pulled into an alley. It was a shady place. He rolled down his window and waved over the couple walking towards the van.

"Hey, the Seventh Day Adventist Church, we're looking for the Seventh Day Adventist Church," he didn't really express himself very well. I didn't think the couple understood what he was saying. So I leaned over and asked them for directions. They looked at both of us and said they didn't know. They were polite and would have been helpful had they known. We must have seemed like quite the pair.

"Maybe we should just go back to where we started from and try the directions over again, look for that landmark the lady told me about," I suggested.

Allan didn't seem to want me to tell him what to do. He was aggravated by me trying to take control of the situation. I decided to just let him do his thing and find it on his own, we had time. It was the first time I saw him get a little perplexed with me. I got the impression he felt like he was the man and it was his duty to find the place.

He made a few turns, and finally, there it was. And we were happy to see it! We parked in the parking lot nearby. We had some time to just hang out for a bit before we went in. We had a smoke and joked around with each other and shared some laughs. The mood was light.

"You know, I think hanging out with you is doing me some good," he told me. That confirmed to me what I had been thinking all along. I felt like I was being a good influence on him, and here he was telling me this. "I think I need to get out of this town, start fresh and make a new life for myself."

"Where would you go?" I asked

"Maybe B.C."

"Yeah, well, then maybe you should, if there's nothing here for you." It felt great to be with someone that I felt like I was having a positive impact on. I could see the good parts of Allan. He had a lot of interesting stories of things he's done, and he had a good sense of humour and a great smile. There was still a light inside of him. My mind was racing a bit. I felt like I had made a buddy, what you call a "fast friend". Sometimes people come into your life and make a big impact on you instantly and I felt like this was one of those moments for me.

"You know, I'll never forget you Allan. I just hope you stay away from that crack shit, and any other drug. You're too good for that. You could get yourself a steady job and find a good girl if you clean yourself up and make some positive changes. I see a very charming and charismatic man in you." I meant every word.

"Yeah, it's too bad you're leavin'. We could've had some good times together. You could've been my rock."

"Yeah, well, I can't stay here. I've got to get to my sister's place. Besides, there's nothing here for me either."

"We could've got a little place, two bedrooms, of course. There's lots of work here. You would've been good company."

"Why don't you come with me, drive with me to Beaverlodge?" I asked him. I was jumping through ideas again, not thinking things through before making suggestions or thinking my thoughts over.

"Really? Well, I don't have enough money to get there."

"I've got the gas money," I was allowing myself to dream up a half-assed plan to get me to where I wanted to go, and to get Allan out of Red Deer. For some reason I thought this would be exciting, keep the adventure going.

"Well, now, wait a minute. Then what would I do?" He asked. Of the two of us, Allan was thinking this through more than me.

"You could get a job there, start a new life." But I was leading Allan down a path that he wasn't meant to take; clearly, just picking up and driving to Beaverlodge, six hours away, with no money wasn't a good idea.

"No, I can't do that." At least Allan thought rationally about it. He had thought about it and knew it wasn't a good thing for him to do. At that point, I would have just kept going with the flow forgetting about my bus ticket and original plan.

I texted Sarah again to let her know where I was.

ME: Hey, Allan and I are about to have dinner at the Seventh Day Adventist Church, see, no worries

Sarah: Erin, why are you hanging out with someone you met on the street, you need to get back to the bus station.

ME: I will, I'm going to.

Sarah: Something is wrong, I don't like the way you're acting right now.

ME: Sarah, Allan and I had a good time today. We're just filling in some time together. It's like we're fast friends.

SarahH: You don't even know him! Of course he's going to be acting like a nice guy, that's what they do!

ME: TRUST ME, Sarah, I'm listening to my instincts on this. Just trust me.

Sarah: I don't trust you right now, you're acting very strange.

ME: Sarah, I'm helping Allan, we're helping each other really. THIS IS MY RELIGION.

Sarah: This isn't right, I really don't like the way you're acting right now. I don't understand.

ME: Just trust me please.

Sarah: Are you still getting on the bus tonight?

ME: Yes, of course.

Sarah: Just make sure you're on that bus. I'm going to keep checking in on you to make sure you get on it.

ME: Okay, don't worry.

Sarah: I am worried

ME: Well, you don't need to, everything is okay.

Sarah: Well, I am.

I felt frustrated. To me it seemed like Sarah just didn't trust me, didn't trust my instincts and wanted me to be like her. She was raining on my parade. I didn't see myself as taking huge risks at the time, I saw it as believing in the good of another human being, even when they're down. I felt caged in by Sarah. Maybe it wasn't what she was saying, maybe it was more how she was saying it. After talking with her I felt like a child who had done wrong and was being scolded by their parents.

I told Allan about Sarah and I and how we're fighting because I'm hanging out with him. I gave him a run down about the dynamic of our relationship; told him how our personalities are basically at the opposite ends of the spectrum, literally. We actually both took the Myers-Briggs Personality test online and found that the only similarity we had was that we were both introverted. But, opposites attract, right?

Maybe I should have just been happy that she cared about me and this is why she was upset. But, at the time I just wanted her to let me be me, even if it was a little bit too free. I didn't think of how this behaviour was affecting her. Of course she was upset. But she wasn't here to see Allan and I hang out. We really did have a good rapport between us, we were having a good time, smiling, laughing, and talking out some personal stuff. I felt like we met each other for a reason that day, and I didn't want to stop hanging out with him because Sarah was mad about it. She wasn't there; she didn't know what it was like.

Allan listened to me and didn't judge what I had to say. He had lived a life where there were no airs about him. Maybe that's one of the reasons why I felt comfortable around him. I didn't have to have a fancy job, a lot of money and a ton of friends to be liked by Allan. Allan liked me in this moment when I was literally at one of the lowest points in my life. And I liked Allan, even though he was at rock bottom of his.

When we got out of the van and walked over to the church across the parking lot, I recognized some of the people lingering outside the door. Some of the natives from the shelter were outside, and they were friendly when they saw us. They smiled and nodded, and some said hello. This must be how groups form on the street, just like everywhere else; if you frequent the same places you wind up getting to know one another.

When we went inside there were long tables laid out horizontally with chairs for people to sit and eat. Allan and I walked over to the serving line where a buffet of food was waiting. The servers were on the other side of the table, dressed in suits and dresses. They smiled a lot and seemed very happy to be offering up this food for us. Sometimes it seems as though spiritual people have a special glow in their eye, a kind of happiness that shines through. We filled our plate with chicken, vegetables, mashed potatoes, gravy and a bun. We even had a bowl of soup as an appetizer. It was a tasty looking home cooked meal.

When Allan and I sat down across from each other to enjoy the feast, we both took some time to look around and check out the scene. There were people scattered about sitting down and eating throughout the whole room. These people were the down and outs of society. Hardly any life was in this room. These were the defeated people, the hopeless people, the homeless people. Some sat with their coats and tuques on while resting their heads on the table to nap after having a meal. Most of the people sat alone. There were some groups, and some conversations going on, but most stayed silent and solo. Allan and I seemed to be an example of the liveliest pair. Allan, of course, with his beaming grin of happiness, simply because he had met a friend today. One person really can make a difference in someone's life.

After Allan had looked around, he said to me, "You know, we should be standing behind the buffet table, not sitting out here."

He was stating that we should change our lives. We should be helping, not being helped. That was a positive statement he made, another sign that perhaps Allan was reflecting on the state of his being.

"I totally agree, Allan." And, I did agree. Helping people has always felt like some sort of calling for me. I just didn't know how to go about doing it. But I wasn't homeless, Allan was. I was in between places while this was actually Allan's life.

Chapter Five – The Drop-Off

After dinner, we went back to the van and smoked a couple cigarettes together. Allan got a phone call. He left the van and went outside to take it.

When he came back he said he had something he had to do. He wanted me to go for a ride with him to do a drop off, a crack drop off.

"No way!" I was serious. "I'm not going anywhere near that place."

"It'll just take a minute," he said. "I promise we won't be there long."

"No, there's no way I'm going, you can drop me off at the bus station first before you go."

Allan really didn't want to drop me off.

"Listen, ah, I have this deal where if I am a runner they give me a little taste, but I won't take any this time, I promise."

"Allan, you're gonna do what you're gonna do, but I don't want any part of it, just drop me off at the station, please."

He seemed really disappointed and torn, but he started the van and headed to the station. There's no way I wanted to be around a drug deal going down, that was way too over the edge for me. Frankly, I had lost hope for Allan's recovery at that point. He was talking earlier about how he wanted to change his life, improve his situation, get away from that kind of scene, and I believed him. I saw the light in him. But, here was the darkness creeping back in before the day had even passed. The first phone call he got he was ready to run.

"This is it, " he said, "I'm not going to take any crack, I'm just going to take the money. I need the money." He was trying to explain himself to me, but even I didn't believe him at this point. I was really disappointed, but what was I to expect, that it would be easy?

"I'm serious, this is different." He told me.

He pulled up in front of the bus station doors. The station had long been closed by now and I was going to have to wait outside the doors with my bags until my bus came. Allan got out to help me.

"Are you going to be here when I get back, I won't be long?" He asked. He really didn't seem like he wanted to leave me. He was going to miss my company.

"The question is, will YOU be back, Allan. I'll be here."

He looked at the station and said, "Listen, why don't I take you to that Tim's across the street. You could sit there and have a coffee, instead of staying out here."

"Okay, sure, that would be better," I said, as we started to put my bags back in the side door of the van. I had about another hour and a half before my bus would come.

When we pulled up to Tim Horton's, we both got out and carried my bags over onto the sidewalk in front of one of the store windows.

"Hey, you should open up that violin of yours and play it. You know, put your case out and try to make some cash while I'm gone."

"Yeah, maybe," I said, but there was no way I felt comfortable doing that. First of all, I didn't even really know how to play this violin. At this point, if I had my guitar I might have tried it. I mean, I'd have nothing to lose, and I was a stranger in this town. But, I didn't have enough balls to act like I knew how to play the violin for money.

"Okay," Allan said, "I'll be right back" With that, he hopped back in the van and pulled out.

I arranged my bags neatly together where they sat and went inside to grab myself a coffee.

By the time I had gotten inside, waited in line for the couple people ahead of me to get served, and ordered my "medium coffee, double double," Allan was back. I didn't see him pull in, but as I was reaching for my coffee and turning to go sit down, I saw him come flying in the door with a big grin on his face.

"That was fast," I said, as he approached me. I hadn't even had a chance to sit down yet.

"I didn't do it," he says, and he looked very proud of himself.

"What, really, wow, good for you!" I was impressed with him too.

"Yeah, I pulled out and started to head that way and then I just thought to myself 'No, I'm not gonna do it', especially not when I have you to hang out with."

"Wow, Allan, I'm really proud of you, good for you!"

He was flying with energy, he felt so proud of himself. I asked him if he wanted a coffee, which he declined, and then we sat down together. I couldn't believe how big he was smiling. I just had to take a picture of him. There he was, sitting across the table from me grinning from ear to ear and shining with exuberance.

I sent the picture to Sarah, and told her Allan and I are at the Tim Horton's across from the bus station. I never got a reply.

We didn't stay in Tim's long. I think we both felt more relaxed and comfortable hanging out in his van. I brought my coffee with me and we went outside. He happily put my belongings back in his van and we just hung out and talked in the parking lot together.

Allan told me more about his past, about the crazy side of his past; about the drugs, the sex, the deals, the fights, the close calls, and the wild and recklessness of it all. I remember thinking his stories fascinated me. It was a glimpse into something I would never live first hand. I liked listening to him; I wish I could remember more of the details.

"You know, I've often thought that someone should write the story of my life," He stated.

"That's funny, cause I've always wanted to write a book." I replied back. And we looked at each other for a minute, pondering it all with smiles on our faces. Maybe we WERE brought together for a reason.

"I could tell you stories, girl." Right away the thought of writing Allan's biography excited me. My mind was pondering ideas of how this could work.

"You have an incredible story. We just need to hang out with each other for a few months so you can tell me your stories and I can write them all down. What if you did come with me to my sister's place. We could hang out, get jobs and write in our spare time." It sounded really exciting to me.

Allan was pretty fired up about it too, but just as before, he needed more of a plan. His wheels were turning though. "Well, now, it would take a lot of time. We need a good chunk of time to just sit and get it all down." He was thinking.

"I would keep it real and make you really happy with how it comes out, I know I would." I was thinking out loud more than anything else. There's nothing more exciting than that initial spark of an idea, when the shine of it glows so bright and so full of new hope. The practicality of that idea doesn't necessarily always follow.

"I'm going to run this idea past Sarah," I said. Why I would think she'd be happy with this idea, I don't know. Apparently I'd let it slip my mind how concerned she already was with my behaviour. I wanted her opinion though. It was true, I had always wanted to write a book, and I have a writing background in journalism. I was schooled, but never used my education. I wanted to write my own stories, and Allan's story really interested me. Sarah knew my creative side. She's heard the songs I have written, read a children's story I had written, and knew I had a dream of writing a book. Maybe she would see that Allan's intriguing tale was a great opportunity for me. Maybe she would help me to work out the details of how to go about it. Maybe she would help me to work out a plan. This time I called her, I wanted to talk to her in person.

"Hello."

"Hey," I greeted her when she answered the phone.

"Where are you?" she asked.

"I'm just at a Tim Horton's. It's right across from the bus station; I can see it from here."

"Are you still getting on the bus?"

"Yes, of course. Listen, I want to run something by you, okay?"

"What," she said.

"Allan and I were just talking, and it turns out that he has always wanted someone to write his story, and, well, you know how I've always wanted to write one! So what do you think about us getting together somehow to write a book?"

"What? Are you serious? You don't even know this guy, now you're going to run off with him and write a book? What is going on with you?" I guess I should have known this would be her reaction.

"Are you getting on that bus or what?" She was pretty serious with me.

"Yes, I'm getting on the bus, I just wanted to know what your opinion was on me possibly getting together with Allan to write a book. I'm a dreamer, I want to believe that these things are possible."

"Well, you're acting really strange, I can't talk to you like this."

"What, I just wanted your opinion."

"Well my opinion is that you should get on that bus and go to your sister's place, not be hanging out with some guy named Allan."

Allan was sitting beside me the whole time Sarah and I were having this conversation. He was not impressed with her reaction. He was kind of shocked by it and thought it was extreme, I could tell by his body language and the look on his face. I was starting to feel a little defensive now. I really thought she was over-reacting.

"Listen, I'm getting on the bus and I'm going to my sister's place, but Allan has a good story so I'm just thinking about maybe taking the time to write it."

"Well, how are you going to do that? You're going to run off with Allan even though you've just met?"

"No, I'm not going to run off with him. I don't know, maybe we could stay in Beaverlodge where my house is." At one time I had a life in Alberta in close proximity to my sister. During those years I bought a little granny house in a tiny town named Beaverlodge. When I moved back to Ontario I kept the house and have been renting it out to an older native lady and her grown son.

"And what, kick your renters out because you want to write a story?"

"No, I don't know, I haven't thought of all the details yet. I just wanted your opinion." I felt exhausted trying to explain myself to her.

Allan tried to say something to me about the situation, but I didn't hear what he said. Sarah heard his voice too.

"Is he right there?" she asked.

"Yes," I answered.

"What? What is going on? I can't talk to you like this. Just get on the bus. Tell me when you're on the bus." She wanted to go, she was done talking to me.

"Okay," I said, feeling like the wind had just been knocked out of my sail.

"Wow, "Allan said, "that's rough."

"Yeah, she's pretty pissed." Allan knew from me telling him earlier that Sarah is a jail guard. "Here, take a picture of my license. Tell her to scan it, I've never been to jail." Allan took out his wallet and pulled out his driver's license. He handed it to me so I could take a picture of it on my phone. I thought this was a very good sign. If Allan was out to hurt me, like Sarah was so worried about, why would he give me his identification card to send to her? He couldn't take me out somewhere to kill me and dump my body off if Sarah knew his full name and what he looked like, he'd be on a wanted list. He'd no longer be anonymous. Besides, I was taking pictures of him throughout the day and sending them to her. If he wanted to do me harm, wouldn't he have resisted not only getting his picture taken in the first place, but also sending it out to a personal friend? So I took a photo of Allan's identification, and I sent it to Sarah.

ME: Here, Allan wants you to know that he's never been in jail before. Here's his photo ID, if you want to check him out at work.

She still wasn't very impressed. She didn't want to talk to me at this point. I felt like we were on the verge of breaking up.

It's hard to describe the feeling in your stomach you get when you know something's not right, but you don't really want to fully realize the truth. I felt defeated. The carpet of the excitement I was standing on was just yanked out from under my feet and I fell flat on my face. Allan was there to pick me up and brush me off. Of course, we had a smoke.

"Man, that was rough, she just wouldn't hear it, eh?" Allan spoke first.

"Yeah, she's pretty pissed right now. I just wanted to run the idea by her. It's not like I'm running off with you. Something came up out of the blue and I wanted to discuss it with her, but she wouldn't even give me the time of day with it. Maybe it would be a cool thing to do. Maybe that's why we met, am I not allowed to believe in the great possibilities life might have to offer?"

"She shut you down pretty hard. And she does not like me one bit."

"She doesn't even know you," I said.

"She thinks she knows me, but she doesn't."

"Well, what are we gonna do Allan? Are we going to figure out a way to write this book or what, what do you think?"

"Well, let's see. We're both really interested in doing it, but it's going to take a big block of time to actually do it. I mean, we'd have to sit down with each other for hours and hours to get it done." He took a drag of his smoke and thought for a minute. "Ok, here's what we'll do. We'll exchange phone numbers, you'll go to your sister's place as planned and we'll keep in touch. We'll think about it, and if we still want to do it at some point in the future we'll find a way to get together and tackle it."

"Sounds like a plan. I know we can't just jump into something like this, but the idea of doing a creative project with someone that has such raw stories as yours is really exciting for me. We plugged each other's numbers into our phones.

"Well, Allan," I said while looking at the time on my phone, "I guess it's time I should be getting over to the bus station." Our time was nearing its end.

"Okay girl," and with that, Allan started the van and took us across the street to wait for the bus to come. We parked around back where we could see when the bus arrived. It wasn't very busy, it seemed like my bus was the only one going out at this time by the looks of the amount of people standing around.

"I want to give you something," I told Allan, as I leaned back between the open space of the two front seats and started to rummage through my duffel bag.

"Oh, no, you don't have to do that," the expression in Allan's voice when he said this was one that was touched. I could tell he wasn't used to gifts of this nature, tokens or reminders of friendship.

"Yes, I want to, this totally reminds me of you and I think you should have it." I pulled out a grey baseball cap with the words AMPED UP written on the front face of it. It even had a lightning bolt symbol underneath it.

"This totally suits you Allan. The whole day you were on a happy high. I'll always remember your big smile and vibrant energy you showed me today. I hope you wear it and remember that you have that great light inside of you and you shouldn't throw it away on drugs." Allan was touched. He said he would wear it with pride.

It's funny, it's just a silly hat, a hat that I had found actually. There was no monetary value attached to it at all, but the meaning of it was priceless. Two souls were brought together today: Two people that experienced a great truth between each other. Allan told me very private, intimate and probably embarrassing things about his life. I was candid about my life with him as well. Neither one of us had anything to lose by doing this, afterall, we were just a couple of strangers hanging out for a day. But the day had been full of meaning, for both of us. And that day was now going to be symbolized for Allan in the form of an AMPED UP grey baseball cap.

"You know Allan, if you had your shit together you'd be quite the catch. In fact, if I was straight I'd be interested in you. You have a charm about you. You're funny and fun to be around. And for an older guy, you're pretty good lookin', especially when the colour comes back into your face." I laughed, as I had teased him a bit in the tail end of what I had just said.

"Really! You really would be interested in me?" Allan seemed kind of shocked by that, and proud at the same time.

"Yeah, of course," I answered. In all honesty I was telling Allan a lie, but a white lie at that. I wouldn't be interested in Allan myself, but I'm sure other women would be if he got his life together. I meant what I said about him being charming and fun, and his smile is really nice to look at. But, what I was trying to do for Allan was to give him another reason to get straight and cleaned up. I wanted him to believe that there were better things out there for him than what he was doing. I just wanted Allan to believe in better things for himself.

The bus pulled in. "Well, let's get your stuff on that bus," Allan said, taking charge of taking care of me.

He opened his door and went around to my side to open up the sliding door to take my bags out for the last time. I got out and carried the lighter of the two bags. We brought them over to the bus driver who was standing outside the bus doors.

"Ticket, please." He said.

I showed him my ticket to Grande Prairie and Beaverlodge. He marked my bags for Beaverlodge and told me he'll be leaving in about 15 minutes.

"Okay," I said. "We'll be waiting right over there in that van."

One last smoke with Allan, I was going to miss him. I did feel alive with him, I felt adventurous.

"Well girl, are you going to try and get some sleep on that bus?"

"I hope so, I'm going to be on it all night. I don't get to Beaverlodge until six in the morning."

"Well, I hope you get some rest."

"Me too!" I said. I looked on Allan's dashboard and admired his orange county choppers BIC lighter. I took it in my hands and looked at the picture of the motorcycle on it. I don't know what it is about motorcycles that symbolize freedom more than any other ride, but they do, and everyone knows it.

"Hey, Allan, can I keep this lighter?" I asked.

"Sure," he said, without having to think about it.

"Cool, thanks." Now I had a symbol to remember Allan by. It was a fitting symbol at that. I still have the lighter to this day. I wonder if he still has the hat.

People were starting to get on the bus. "Well, I guess it's time," I said to Allan; time to say goodbye.

For the last time, I got out of his van. We slowly walked over to the front of the bus. People were lined up to get on. Allan and I stood next to each other and waited for the bus to get loaded. I was the last one. We smiled at each other and gave each other a hug. It was a warm and friendly hug.

"Bye Allan," I said as I looked at him after we hugged.

"Bye girl, have a good trip."

"I will, thanks for today."

"Thank you," he said. How do you say goodbye to someone like Allan? I gave my ticket to the bus driver and got on the bus.

Chapter Six – The Breakdown

The bus was packed. I walked up the aisle all the way to the back with my violin in hand and saw that every double seat had someone sitting in it. Nobody wants to share a seat with a stranger on a greyhound bus, especially not on a long ride. You can feel people thinking to themselves as you walk by "please don't pick this seat". They just look at you with a frown on their face. Quite frankly, I didn't want to sit with anyone else either. Bodies were strewn out over the seats getting ready for a snooze and people had their knapsacks placed on the aisle seat beside them, as they were snuggly tucked in by the window. When I got to the back of the bus, I turned around. The front seat was open. That was my only option if I was going to have a seat to myself. So I walked up to the front of the bus and sat down in the very first row on the right hand side of the driver. I had the best view of all with the wide open road laying straight ahead of me.

I was alone again, but felt good to be on the road to my sister's place. I was going to see my family and that gave me a warm feeling in my belly.

I got myself settled into my front row seat. I tried to put my violin up in the baggage cart above my head, but it was too awkward to fit in there. I didn't mind snuggling up with my violin beside me. It almost felt like it gave me strength somehow anyway. It let people know that I was a musician. It was a badge of honour for me, just like wearing a uniform is a badge of honour for a police officer. My violin spoke of creativity, emotion, and beauty. I was proud to have it sit next to me.

I texted my sister and let her know I was on the bus safe and sound. She got back to me and confirmed the time she would be picking me up in the morning. Then I texted Sarah and let her know I was sitting on the bus. She was glad, told me to try and get some sleep, and to let her know when I got to my sister's place.

It was time for me to try and settle down to rest for the long ride. It was a Saturday night at 9:30pm, and all I wanted to do was be able to sleep.

I watched as the young bus driver, who had to be around the same age as me in his early thirties, pulled out of the bus terminal. We only had to drive through Red Deer briefly before we hit the highway towards Edmonton. I said my goodbyes to Red Deer, knowing I probably would never be back, and grateful for the experiences I had while there. The lights of the city grew smaller behind me.

There's something about being on the open road. It's the in-betweenness of life. Not really being anywhere, but being somewhere at the same time. It's the having been, and the going to. It's a break. I liked sitting and looking out the window at the scenery, even though it was dark, but I could see the road ahead, the land lying near the edges and the stars in the sky. It was a clear beautiful night.

I finally tried to close my eyes and rest. It's not like I wasn't tired, but sleep was still very much elusive. My eyes were closed, but my mind was open. Thoughts were travelling through, bringing me to the past, the present and wondering about the future. I thought about Allan, Sarah, my family, my mother, my father, my life, things I'd done in the past, what I wanted to do in the future, philosophy of living, and the world in general. I was calm, but not still. There was no hope of rest for me. I was beginning day 4 of no sleep.

So I opened my eyes and gave up the idea of falling asleep. Besides, I was resting, it's not like I was doing any sort of rigorous activity. I was just sitting on a bus as distance and time passed me by.

When I grew tired of looking out the window, like most people, I took out my phone and looked through my facebook feeds. At least it was a way to get out of my thoughts and check out what was on other people's minds at some point in time. I'm not really a social feed kind of person though, so my time spent doing that wasn't very satisfying. I started to think about Sarah, and what our relationship is like. I read through the texts we had sent each other while I was in Red Deer and pondered on the meaning of them. I was tired of arguing.

As I put my phone away I settled into looking out the front window again. I leaned forward and rested my arms crossed on the metal bar in front of my seat that separated me from the three stairs that led down to the door. I took a deep breath and concentrated on relaxing.

The bus driver was really close to me. If I leaned over and reached out with my left arm I could touch him. Here we were, a couple of strangers sitting on a long bus ride together with no one to talk to even though we were sitting right next to each other. I found human relationships strange sometimes. We keep ourselves at a distance. Maybe it's a protection mechanism, maybe it's just silly.

I wanted to break the ice with him. I wasn't sure how, but I felt like even though we were strangers we should still be able to have a conversation.

"It's a nice night, eh?" I might as well start with simple pleasantries.

He looked back at me with a quick glance, "Yes, it sure is" he responded. He didn't seem bothered if I was going to try and talk with him. After all, he was just hanging out driving by himself for hours.

"I love checking out the night sky," I commented.

"So do I," he said, "I especially like watching the moon."

"Me too."

"Like tonight, the moon looks so far away, yet it's almost full." I looked out the front window and spotted the moon a way off and upward to the left in the night sky.

"It was a full moon a couple of nights ago, now it's waning." I said.

"Waning? What's that." He asked.

"When the moon is waxing, its growing in size towards its full moon state and when it wanes it's getting smaller. Since it was full a couple nights ago, it's starting to wane a little."

The driver nodded his head in understanding. "So do you know why it looks so far away right now?" He really was interested in the sky. I was glad to be having this conversation.

"Um, I can't say for sure. But I would guess it has something to do with the earth's axis and rotation."

"Makes sense," he said. "My favourite is the Harvest moon."

"Yeah, that's a beauty."

"You know why they call it the Harvest moon?" He asked me.

"Something to do with the season," I said.

"Yeah, it's the last full moon closest to the autumn equinox. In the old days farmers used to use the light of the moon to harvest their crops by it. It was important back in the day when there weren't any lights on their tractors."

"That's cool," I said. I liked being taught new knowledge like that, I found it interesting.

"You ever see the northern lights?" I asked him.

"Just once, it was mostly just shimmering green light, and it didn't last for very long."

"Boy, I saw a show once."

"Like what?"

"Well, I was at my sister's place, which is where I'm headed now. I used to live out here in the Beaverlodge area for almost 7 years. One time I was at Christine's place and we were out having a campfire. It was late, probably about 1 or 2 in the morning when they started. They just came all of a sudden. We looked up into the sky and saw shivering white light. The light was dancing from one spot of the sky to another spot beside itself, flickering back and forth. Then, as well as dancing back and forth it began to take shapes. We saw the shimmering white light transform into animal shapes, then it would collapse in on itself and jet across the sky to the left a bit and transform into another shape. We were in awe of what we were seeing. All we could say was 'Wow'. Then it stopped."

"That would have been pretty amazing to see," the bus driver commented.

"Yeah, it was. I saw them one more time at Christine's house, again late at night at a campfire. This time when we looked up we saw the white lights create something like a cathedral ceiling. There was a centre point in the middle, and from there the lights branched out in streams all around us. It was pretty cool to see too."

"I bet," he said. "You know what the northern lights are?" He asked. It seemed like he was a bundle of information, which I liked.

"Vaguely, my uncle explained it to me once but it didn't all stick with me."

"It's particles from the sun colliding with gaseous particles from the earth."

"Hmm, how does that happen?" I was intrigued.

"Electrons and Protons from the sun are blown towards the earth. The reason the northern lights only happen near the north and south poles is because the magnetic force of the earth is weaker there, so the particles can be blown into our atmosphere, and when they collide with gas particles it creates the dancing light we see."

"Wow, eh, it's all pretty amazing when you think about it."

"Yes, it sure is." He said, as a moment of silence fell upon us. He was a clean cut, articulate and well groomed man.

"So, are you just heading to your sister's for a visit?" He asked.

"Well, not exactly. I sort of changed my plans recently."

"Oh, yeah, how so?"

I told him how I was planning on planting trees here in Northern Alberta for the spring and summer; that I had an old friend who is still in the business from my older days from when I planted when I was younger. I planted for four seasons in a row when I was in my early twenties.. My friend runs her own crew now. She called me up this winter and asked me to come on out and plant this year with her crew, she also needed some help with staffing since her right hand woman wasn't going to be returning. It seemed like perfect timing for me. I was working a job I was completely bored with and thought it would be nice to go back out west for the summer, see some old friends and sock some money away in the bank. So I went for it. I felt like I needed a break from my life, and if Sarah and I were meant to be together we'd make it through one summer apart.

I told him how when I got out here, however, it turned out to be a different story for me. All of a sudden I was unsure of my decision. I was staying at my friend's cabin, which I loved and thought it was so cute and thoroughly enjoyed the scenery around me, but something had changed. I was in a different phase of my life. My friend was still in the same phase, we had grown apart.

The first night we got together I met her and Sam, someone who had been working for her for the last few seasons, at the airport. The reunion was really nice, we were both happy to see each other and hugged hello. I had put my bags in the back of her little pick-up truck, and off we went headed to Rocky Mountain House a little ways outside of Calgary. It felt familiar and nomadic, something I was used to.

I told the bus driver about the beers in the truck on our way to Diamond's cabin, and how we drank all night as a reunion to seeing each other again. I didn't tell him that something was different about me that night; something I didn't even know was lingering around just yet.

As the next couple of days passed, I told him that I was really feeling like I wanted to go home. My friend drank every day, and I didn't want to be in that environment all the time. I couldn't do it, it wasn't healthy for me, and I didn't want to be the stick in the mud either.

I didn't tell him that I couldn't sleep the whole three nights I was there, or that I stopped taking my Cipralex, antidepressant medication, because I was scared I couldn't keep track of it. But I did tell him that I was having serious doubts whether I wanted to commit my whole summer to tree planting again.

"It's hard work," he said. Everyone says that, and it's absolutely right. It's the hardest and most physically and mentally challenging job I've ever had. Mentally challenging because you have to stay motivated and aware of what you're doing, physically because you're carrying 50 lbs. bags of trees on your hips while trekking through an old logging site in the woods for 12 hours a day planting one tree at a time, 2000+ times a day. Rain or shine, it's planting time.

I told the bus driver how I missed my comfort place, I missed my home, and I missed my girl. I missed my daily shower routine at Diamonds's place. She had a shower, but I felt like if I wanted to use it every day I was being a wimp. I wasn't in treeplanter mentality mode, and I wasn't sure I wanted to be. I must have changed a little over the years. I didn't want to give up all of my creature comforts, even though I still have a great deal of love for wilderness and the great outdoors. The bus driver completely understood and didn't question at all why I chose not to stick it out.

There were moments when I wanted to stay and tough it out. Like when Diamond took me into town to check out the local music store. That's where I bought my violin. I figured I would learn how to play it at night after planting, just like I had done with my guitar years earlier. But, those moments were fleeting. For the most part, I felt out of place and seriously re-considering my decision. Every night I was kept up with worry-some thoughts, tossing and turning until early morning. I would call Sarah just to hear her voice and talk to someone who I felt loved me. Diamond kept saying a few times that I seemed spaced out and not normal too.

Sam played the guitar, and at first I thought it would be fun to be in an environment with another musician. But when we were hanging out throughout the day and he went off to go practice, I watched him from a distance and thought how lonely a musician's life really is. I used to do what he was now doing. I used to spend hours practising my music and dreaming of becoming a performer. But when I looked out the porch window and saw him playing his heart and soul out across the lawn sitting on a stump all by himself, the charm of it was officially over for me. I was done spending a lot of time on something that I was doing nothing with. My interests were changing, and his interests are what mine used to be. I had grown past this phase of my life, and now I felt like I was looking back at it first hand from a different perspective.

I just wanted to get to my sister's place, and think about whether or not I should stick to planting for the summer. I wanted to get to what I considered to be a comfort zone; a place where I could relax more, and possibly sleep through the night.

So, while we are now travelling on this bus, dear reader, let me tell you more about what happened to get us here. This is how I ended up spending the day on the street in Red Deer with Allan not knowing the whole while that my mind was teetering on the edge of reality.

After the third day at Diamond's cabin, I let her know that I was reconsidering going out to camp this year. She understood, and we looked into the bus schedule out of Red Deer to see when I could catch a bus to Christine, my sister's, neck of the woods. We made a plan that I would take her truck into Red Deer in the morning and I would leave it in the parking lot at the bus station until she rolled through on her way to Beaverlodge. Beaverlodge, where my house is and where the owners of the tree planting company live. The married couple are one of my sister's country neighbours. It was a plan. I just had to make it through the night.

Diamond had invited another old tree planting buddy out to her place that day. He lived in Red Deer now, and hadn't planted for a couple of seasons. She was trying to get him to come out and plant again for another season, but he had a steady job working for a grain company. He said he would love to, but he can't. His life had moved on as well. It seemed as though Diamond always wanted people around her so they could drink. It had been three days, and that's what happened. It's fun for a while, but not for long for me. I wasn't partaking, I was trying to gather my stuff up and get ready for my ride out in the morning. I had to leave early if I was going to make it on time. So, I said my goodbyes that night, and went out to the motor home to try to catch my sleep.

I gave it a valiant effort, but the idea of having to get up early and catch a bus was on my mind. I couldn't get settled. It was about three in the morning and I'd had enough of lying in bed tossing and turning. That was it; I was just going to take off now.

I went inside the cabin, and just as they were when I had left hours earlier, Diamond and the boys were still up partying. I told her that, again, I couldn't sleep and I want to just leave now and get the drive over with. She asked me if I was sure. I just explained that I'm wired, there's no way I can rest, so what's the use of me lying there not being able to sleep. I might as well just hit the road while I'm up anyway.

"Okay, if that's what you want to do" she was pretty easy going about it.

"Here, take a couple of Red Bulls for the ride," the guy from Red Deer said.

"Thanks, that's nice of you." I said my goodbyes again, and took off.

I was fine on the highway, but as soon as I got into Red Deer, that's when I realized how tired I was. I had simple instructions on how to get to the bus station. The first turn I came to, however, I found I couldn't think straight. It was hard for me to calculate the lights and the turn at the same time. Quite frankly, I had reached exhaustion, and I knew I had to get myself off the street and park somewhere safe and try to get some serious rest before I drove again. I wanted to make it to the bus station to park, but my driving was horrible, my decision-making was not there and I was a hazard on the road.

I turned into the first parking lot I found, and stayed there. I pushed the seat back and closed my eyes. It was cold, dark and really early in the morning. I had a few hours before my bus left, so I felt okay for time. At least I wasn't worried about missing it anymore. It felt nice to close my eyes and to be safely off the road. I stayed there for about half an hour with my eyes closed. I didn't sleep, but at least I took some time to regroup my brain a little. Afterwards, I decided to try and make it the rest of the way to the bus station. I felt a little more refreshed and ready to tackle the whole driving thing again. It's really amazing how much sleep deprivation affects our thoughts and actions; what we take for granted to be simple suddenly becomes difficult.

When I got back on the road, I thought I was heading in the right direction. I must have been, there was only one turn to take and then I could follow the bus station signs on the road, but where were the signs? I really question my sense of direction sometimes, and this particular time was more than just a little frustrating. I just wanted to get to the station. I must have gone too far. I turned around, looking for the road I missed, or the sign I missed. I drove all the way back to the road I had come in on and tried it again to find the road I was to take, or a bus terminal sign to follow. I don't know how I got lost, I guess realistically nobody knows how they get lost, but I definitely was. I felt like I was going around in circles and I was ready to scream my head off with frustration. That's when I saw a sign to Edmonton.

I don't know why, but I could have sworn that Diamond had said to me that if I wanted to keep going to Edmonton that would be fine. She had to go through there anyway when she heads out for work, so I could leave her truck at the bus station there. That's what I thought, anyway. So, instead of being lost in Red Deer, I chose to get back on the main highway and head towards Edmonton. Like I said, I could have sworn that Diamond and I had talked about it earlier.

I checked my gas gauge, it read over half a tank. I made my decision. Edmonton, here I come. I knew Edmonton more than I knew Red Deer. I had never been to Red Deer, but I had been to Edmonton several times. I figured it would be easier for me to maneuver in a more familiar city. Rationality wasn't my strong suit at this point in time, but I was completely unaware of it.

I thought it was going to be smooth sailing to Edmonton. It was early with hardly any traffic and it was straight highway driving without any turns. But I didn't get too far.

Shortly after I had turned onto the highway heading towards Edmonton, the truck lost its power. It slowed down to a crawling halt on the side of the road. I was stranded on the highway. I tried to start it again, but no go. The lights would turn on, but it wouldn't start. Damn! That's all I need, I thought to myself. I tried to stay calm and think this through. I really hope I didn't blow her engine or something. I hope it didn't need oil or something serious. I popped the hood to take a look at the oil dipstick. I got out, walked to the front of the truck and opened the hood. There wasn't any smoke, so I thought that was a good sign. I looked around to find where the oil stick was, and found it after a few seconds. I pulled it out and wiped it off. There was oil to wipe off, so it can't be too low. When I stuck it back in and pulled it out again I saw oil on the tip, which I was very grateful to see. Other than that, I didn't know what to do. I didn't know what the problem was.

I closed the lid and got back in the driver's seat. With a last Hail Mary turn of the key I hoped it would miraculously start, but no go. I was stranded, and I thought I better stop trying to start it before I drain the battery too.

That was the straw that broke the Camel's back for me. The breakdown of the truck released the dam inside of me that was holding my emotions together and I cried like I'd never cried before. I blubbered in tears on the side of the highway in the middle of nowhere like a baby. The breakdown had caused a breakdown. I had had enough.

I allowed myself to cry out every last tear and drain my body to a feeling of numbness. Then I sat still in the remnants of my tears, sniffles, and body shakes. I knew I had to call Diamond, but I didn't want to, not yet. I'm sure nobody likes to be caught in a moment like this, stranded and alone needing to call for help. So I put off making that phone call for the moment. Instead, I called Sarah for support.

Luckily there is a two hour difference in time between where I was in Alberta and where Sarah was in Ontario. It was earlier in the morning for me, but approaching a more reasonable hour to call her.

When she answered the phone, I broke down again when I tried to explain to her where I was and what had happened. She was very gentle with me, and I could feel her love for me. I was so grateful to be talking to her and I couldn't wait to get home to her. This was one of those times when I felt so much love for her and from her that it took away the fact that we often fought.

"Are you okay?" she asked me.

"Yes, I just needed to talk to you before I call Diamond," I said through my tears. My throat was welling up again. Sarah was my rock, she was my safe place.

"Well, you have to call her," she said.

"I know, I just needed to take a moment."

"Do you want me to talk to her?"

"No, I'll do it. I just don't know how good of friends we are anymore and I'm a little nervous to call her up and tell her I'm stranded on the highway."

"What do you mean you don't know how good of friends you are anymore?"

"Well, I just don't know if she really likes me anymore," I said.

"Erin, you think that about everybody." Sarah stated. It was true. I was often insecure about other's thoughts about me. It's almost as if I'd let myself develop a slight negative paranoia as to how they were thinking about me judging by what I saw of their body language and tone of voice. I never used to be like that, but somehow I allowed myself to feel unliked by others.

"I know, but I don't think we're friends anymore."

"Erin, it's probably just in your head. You better call her so she can come and get you, okay?" Sarah liked to get things done.

"Okay, I will, right now"

"Okay, text me and let me know how it's going."

"I will," I said, as we said goodbye and hung up.

I took a moment, saw some traffic speed by, and then I made the phone call. But there was no answer. I hung up and tried calling back right away. Again, there was no answer, just the answering machine. I knew Diamond was there, she had just been up drinking late into the night and they were all passed out now in her cabin. I needed to wake them up. So, I called back again for a third time, this time I left a message. I let her know that I was stranded in her truck on the highway and I needed her to call me right away soon as she got up.

I let some time pass, then I texted Sarah to let her know I can't get a hold of Diamond . Sarah took it upon herself to call her, she wasn't shy.

A little while later I got a call from Sarah. "You know, you've got a real friend in Diamond. She really cares about you. And she's on her way."

"How do you know she cares about me?" I asked.

"Because of the way she talks about you. Everything is fine, you don't have to worry. She's on her way soon with her Dad."

"Thanks Sarah, I don't know what I'd do without you. I love you."

"I love you too. Now, you should save your phone battery in case you need it."

"Okay, I'll let you know when I'm at the station."

"Okay, bye, love you."

"Love you too, Sarah, bye."

I got out of the truck to stretch my legs and move around a bit. That's when I realized I had a bunch of empty beer cans floating around in the back of the truck. The last thing I needed was a cop to spot me on the highway with a bunch of old beer cans floating around. So, I thought I better do something about it. I got an old plastic bag out of the back and stuffed as many cans as I could in it. It wasn't enough. There was an old beer box that took the rest of the incriminating evidence. Now, we all know Alberta is flat when you're away from the mountains and this spot I was stranded in by the highway was no exception. I could see for miles. There really wasn't anywhere for me to put these cans that wouldn't be an eyesore, I just didn't want them out in the open in the box of the truck I was driving.

I walked towards the ditch toting the beer cans up to where there was a bed of water, it was fairly wide and slow running. I didn't really think it through when I threw a can out there. It just floated across the top of the water, slowly moving out to the centre. I had put three in the water before I stopped myself with the ridiculousness of my actions. Remember, lack of sleep does funny things to your thinking process. I looked around and saw the truck parked on the highway, right next to where I was standing off in the ditch, and now there were three beer cans floating along the water. This wasn't good, I thought. Where am I going to put these cans? Maybe I should just put them back in the truck. No, I can't do that. I left the cans down by the water. I figured if a cop came by and questioned me about them I could just say I didn't know anything about it. He can't prove they were in my truck. I climbed back up the ditch and went and sat in the truck to wait for Diamond.

As I was sitting in the truck I started to feel better about the situation I was in. It was as though my mind forgot about the immediacy of my situation and it started to daydream about what I wanted to do with my life. There I was, stranded on the highway, and I was thinking about writing. I suppose this sounds very impractical, but to me it felt as though I was having some sort of revelation. I had always thought of writing in the back of my mind. But at this moment in time it felt like a pressing urge. I looked in the glove compartment box to see if I could find something to write with. I found a pencil. I always carried a journal with me, so I had lots of paper. I began to write. I was interrupted by a text.

Sarah: Has Diamond called you yet?

ME: Not yet.

Sarah: What are you doing?

ME: I'm writing.

Sarah: You're writing? You should be trying to get a hold of Diamond, and find out where she is.

ME: I will, you said she was on her way.

Sarah: Yes, but you need to let her know where you are.

ME: Okay, I will

Sarah: Okay, let me know what's going on.

ME: Okay

I don't know why, but I thought Sarah would be impressed by me wanting to write. I guess the reality was that I had better things to be thinking about at this point in time. But I felt inspired, and there was nothing else I could really do but wait anyway. I didn't try to call Diamond. I figured she would call me when she was ready. She knew the situation, what would me calling her again really accomplish? I would wait for her to call me.

A little while later, my phone rang. "Hello," I answered. It was Diamond.

 "Hi," she said. "Sarah called me."

 "Yeah, she told me."

"She sounded worried about you." It was the tone in her voice that made me feel not at ease. To me, she sounded irritated, and annoyed. Which, I suppose, she had every right to feel. I was trying to remember what Sarah told me about Diamond being a true friend of mine, and that she cares. But, I couldn't quite shake how I really felt.

"So, where are you?" she asked.

"I'm not far out of Red Deer, on the highway headed towards Edmonton."

"Are you sure?"

"Yes, I got turned around in Red Deer and thought I remembered you saying I could go through to Edmonton if I wanted to. So, when I got lost, I decided to go there instead."

"Ah, no, I never said that."

"Really? I thought you did."

"Ah, no, I didn't" she sounded definite. I was in no position to argue, even though I could swear we had that conversation. "I said the bus would take you through to Edmonton, but I didn't say to drive there with my truck."

"Oh, I'm sorry, I thought you did." I really wish I wasn't stuck in this situation. I just want to go home. "I had a huge breakdown cry," I told her.

"Oh, yeah," she said, without an ounce of sympathy. "Well, I'm on my way, and I'll be there within the hour."

"Okay, thank you Diamond."

"Don't worry about it, I'll be there soon. I'll call you when I get closer."

I texted Sarah and let her know that I had talked to Diamond. And I waited.

Time seemed to be other-worldly. I was lost in thought and feeling low and completely drained. It was calming for me to sit in silence, alone, as the time passed. Cars and trucks would race by me, but the highway wasn't very busy at this time.

Finally, I decided I should get a good bearing on where I am so I could relay that information to Diamond when she got closer. I looked around for any landmarks I could use to describe where I was. Far off to the right, in the distance, there was a subdivision. Other than that, there was only an open field and highway. Straight ahead a few miles, there was a bridge overpassing this highway I was on. There was a green sign on the right side of the highway a kilometer or so ahead of me. I couldn't read the sign from where I was, so I decided to get out of the truck and walk up to where I could read it.

The wind was a little chilly. Vehicles zoomed by me at great speed. The limit is often 110 km/hour in Alberta. I was getting closer to being able to read the sign ahead of me.

My phone rang. It was Diamond. "Hello," I answered.

"Hey, we're almost there. So, can you give me some specifics as to where you are? Any landmarks around you?"

"Well, I should be on the highway headed towards Edmonton. There's a subdivision far off on my right hand side. I'm on a split, two lane highway, there's a bridge overpass ahead of me and I'm just walking up to read the sign that's ahead of me." I felt like I was on a mission. I felt like I was proving myself to be in control of the situation and that I was handling it well.

When I got close enough to read the sign, I told Diamond what it said. It was a rectangular green sign with a white dividing line in the middle of it. Both the top and the bottom box had a word written in it, neither words sounded familiar to me. I read them to Diamond, and hoped this would help. They sounded like they could be places, or names of something, but I wasn't sure what.

"Okay, see you soon," she said.

I turned to walk back to the truck when I spotted something in the ditch. It was a hat. I don't usually pick things up that I find lying on the side of the road, but I walked over towards it to get a better look. It was a grey baseball cap, and when I picked it up it looked to be in pretty good shape. The words "AMPED UP" were written on it, with a lightning bolt underneath them. I thought this would be a good souvenir of this horrible time I was stranded on the highway in Alberta. So, I kept it, and carried it with me on my way back to the broken down truck. Little did I know that I would soon meet a man named Allen to whom I would give this to wholeheartedly.

I was still heading back when Diamond and her Dad pulled up behind the truck I had been driving. I was still pretty far away. They got out, and went to the back of their truck to grab something. I kept walking in the wind, with traffic passing me by.

When I got up to the truck, Diamond and her Dad were heading towards it. Diamond had a jerry can of gas in one hand. They were both looking at me as I walked over to the front of the truck, as I looked at them. There was no greeting, Diamond held her head down a little so as not to make eye contact with me. Her dad did all the talking, and stood in between us. He looked at me with a stern face and asked me if I had put gas in the truck. I told him the last time I looked at the gauge it was half empty.

"And when was that," he snapped at me. Clearly he didn't think much of me.

"I checked before I left Red Deer," I said.

He stepped beside me and opened up the driver's side door of the truck. He looked at the gas gauge.

"It says empty," he told me.

"Well, that's because the truck is off, here, I'll turn the key over and look," I said.

"NO! Don't try to start it."

I looked at Diamond, who was keeping her head down, in a kind of feeble way while she was pouring the gas from the jerry can into the truck tank.

I looked at both of them, feeling defeated and humiliated. I turned away and took a few steps in front of the truck. I breathed deeply and tried to stop myself from allowing tears to well up in my eyes. When I felt a little more collected, I turned around and went back to the truck.

Diamond had finished filling the tank and her Dad was getting into the truck to try and start it. With the first turn of the key, it started up with no problems. It was the gas. But I had checked it back in Red Deer before I got on the highway. Didn't I? Maybe the gas gauge didn't work. There were a lot of other little things wrong with this truck. The interior lights won't turn off when the truck is shut down unless the back driver's side door is opened and shut. There were weird glitches all throughout it. When Diamond sent me off in it she gave me a rundown of them all. But she hadn't mentioned the gas gauge. So, did it work? Or did I screw up even more than I had realized? Regardless, I was looking like a big fool, and feeling like one too.

Her Dad was still sitting in the driver's seat when I went over to him to apologize. I told him that I know I really screwed up, and I was sorry. He seemed to be able to tell that I was sincere. I will never know what he was thinking, I can only imagine.

No more time was wasted chit-chatting. Diamond's father said he would follow us into town to the bus station. Diamond got in the driver's seat of her truck, and I walked over and got in on the passenger side. We had to get turned around so we could head back the way I had come.

I wasn't paying attention to where we were going. I didn't realize it, but I must have been acting kind of out of the ordinary. I was concerned with trying to make conversation with Diamond, more than just sitting and heading back to town.

"Your Dad seems pretty pissed," I mentioned to her.

"Nah, he's alright."

"What did he say when you told him what happened?"

"My dad is pretty laid back. He's like me. I'm pretty close to him, so he was like 'Road Trip'."

"Oh, yeah, that's pretty cool. Listen, thanks for coming to get me, I'm sorry about it all."

"Don't worry about it," she seemed to be pretty relaxed with the whole thing. I was the one who was uncomfortable and awkward.

I looked at her and couldn't help but think about how much she reminded me of my littlest brother. I couldn't tell you now why I thought that at the time, but at that moment it was an overwhelming feeling of mine. I told her she reminded me of him. I also told her how I would like to find out what her personality profile was and that there are tests online that I could send her that I would like her to take. She just took everything I said in stride, and simply told me she's not the type to take those kinds of tests. I told her how I knew she would find someone someday. Diamond had just recently told me while I was still at her cabin that she was afraid she wasn't ever going to meet anyone. So, I took my final moments with her to try and reassure her that this wasn't going to be the case. That someday when the time is right she would find someone to share her life with. Diamond simply listened to me talk.

Looking back on it now, I realize how messed up I must have sounded and how illogical my thoughts were at the time. It was as though I had forgotten the situation I was just in and now I was simply living in the moment trying to make conversation with an old friend. I didn't quite comprehend what was going on, I just was.

When we got to the bus station, Diamond got out of the truck and turned around to face her dad parked behind us. She put her hands in the air and jumped up and down in a sort of victory style. I knew then she and I weren't close anymore. I took the victory jumps to heart and figured it was because she was happy to get rid of me.

We got all my gear out of the truck and left it in a pile on the sidewalk by the door to the station. Diamond and her father stood side by side to say our goodbyes. I walked over to Diamond and gave her a hug. Then I looked at her father and gave him a hug as well.

"Good luck," he said, as I pulled away. By the way he said, I could tell he thought I would need it. And with that, Diamond got in her truck and her dad got in his. They were off on their next adventure, and I was left to mine.

I brought my bags inside the bus station to a back room where I could leave them semi safely. Then I decided to find a grocery store so I could get some breakfast and some juice.

And that, dear reader, is where you met me walking down the street in Red Deer. But now, we are on the bus on route to see my sister and her family where I really end up losing a hold on reality. The moment we shall return to however is the present. Presently I am feeling excessively chatty with the bus driver.

Chapter Seven – The End of the Road

I didn't tell the bus driver all these details of my trip so far. But I did tell him about meeting Allan, and how that caused a fight between my girlfriend and I. That's what was on my mind now, and so that's what I talked about.

"Here, you want to know the whole story?" I said. "It's all right here on my phone; I could read you the texts. I'll read them to you if you promise to give me your honest opinion on the matter." I had nothing to lose; I would probably never see this guy again.

"Sure, I've got nothin' but time." He seemed genuinely interested.

So, there we were, driving along on a dark highway in the middle of the night somewhere between Edmonton and Grande Prairie. I had the bus driver's full attention, and his interest was piqued. He was about to get a personal inside view into a lesbian relationship.

"Do you mind if I come and kneel beside you to read them?" I asked.

"No, not at all," he answered. So I got up from my seat and knelt down right beside him. It was close, but it didn't feel too close for comfort. I was glad to be getting a second opinion on what had gone on between Sarah and I while I was in Red Deer. And I felt like I was getting special treatment from the driver.

I read him the dialogue of texts that had gone on between Sarah and I ever since I met Allan. I explained to him what it was like for me to hang out with Allan, and that Sarah was upset with me about it the whole time. He listened to the complete unedited text story from beginning to end. I know he was interested because he would make comments throughout or ask me questions about certain details. He was just as into listening to me read these texts as I was into reading them to him.

After the whole story was aired and I was finished reading, I asked him what he thought. I told him how I was frustrated with Sarah, and how Sarah was frustrated with me. And I didn't know what to make of it.

"Hmm," he said with a thoughtful moment. I waited patiently enough for him to come to some sort of conclusion.

Since I was finished reading, I got up and went and sat back down in my front seat close to the edge so I could hear what he was going to say. The endless road ahead of us kept coming as we travelled along.

"You guys are total opposites. But sometimes that works." He said.

"She needs to feel in control of everything, and I like to just go with the flow. Sometimes her need to control her environment impinges on my need to feel at ease in mine."

"Well, you're definitely very different people." He went on to tell me about a guy he once knew, a guy who was a police officer. He basically summed him up into being a total control freak. We both acknowledged that not all cops are like that, but quite a few are. It's as though when they get a badge and a gun, the power goes to their heads.

Sarah wasn't a cop, like I've said before, she was a jail guard. She had to deal with the "assholes of society" on a daily basis. She wanted to be a cop, but her path never went in that direction. She was still in awe of the military though, which was another dream of hers.

I'm disgusted by mankind resorting to killing each other in war rather than resolving the world's problems together rationally and peacefully. Behind every war there is more to the story than we as civilians are told. I believe our military troops believe in protecting our nation, but it saddens me that they are used as pawns to a greater evil that they are not told about. Sarah would fight, I would protest; that about sums up our differences.

I was grateful for the Bus driver's insights. He didn't try to tell me what to do. He just let me know what we should all know, that if you can communicate with your partner you might have a chance. But, if there are such fundamental differences between you, is it worth trying to communicate through? Would it be better to move on and find someone you're more in sync with?

We went on to chit-chat with each other for a little while longer. I found it easy to talk to him. I wasn't feeling shy or reserved at all, quite the opposite. I felt like the world, and everyone in it was at my fingertips.

After a while I sat back in my seat and disengaged myself from the driver. We had enjoyed some social conversation and now it was time to kick back and relax a bit on the ride.

I enjoyed sitting and watching the open road pass me by. Sleep was still out of the question, but I was at peace nonetheless. Time was passing by. Most of the patrons on the bus were sleeping. It was silent except for the roar of the tires on the pavement and the swish of any passing vehicle on the highway.

This might be a good time to tell you, dear reader, a bit about the days when I used to live out this way. I was searching for something at that time, but I didn't know what. So that's when I started my long list of jobs. I would work a job for a year, thinking I was doing it to get myself out of my student loan debt and by then I would know what I wanted to do with my life. I stayed out west in Alberta in the same area as my sister and her family. She was my rock. She was more than a big sister to me; she was also my mother figure. I fell in love with all of her children and loved being their aunt.

There were a lot of good paying jobs in Alberta, and they were easy to come by. I had some jobs handed to me because some of Christine's neighbours needed help. It was definitely another world out there than what I was used to back home. Christine warned me that it wasn't like Toronto, that the people out here were much more conservative. But, I was a country girl at heart. I had only been a tourist in Toronto anyway. I grew up in the country and that's where I belonged.

As the years passed for me out in Alberta, I had done well for myself in one sense. I had paid off my student loans, bought myself a little house, and I had acquired many skills. I had worked as a Carpenter's Helper, I was trained as a Tilesetter, and I had begun my first year as a Welding Apprentice, where the big money was at. In my spare time I worked on my house and spent time with my sister and her family. I had lived lots of life in the seven years I had been out there. But I suffered through it as well.

I had isolated myself from any kind of social life, not feeling capable of making friends. It's not like I didn't have people I could have been friends with, it was that I was incapable of holding a friendship for long. I felt down on the inside and not good enough, even though I could learn how to do most things, I was never good enough. So, I kept more and more to myself. I didn't like to answer my phone and I didn't always like having to go to the store to get my groceries or other odds and ends. There were times when people would knock on my door and I wouldn't answer. I wasn't trying to be anti-social, in fact I was very lonely, but I would feel anxious when I was presented with a social opportunity. Some of the only times I interacted with people was at work, and even then, being a Tile Setter I worked alone most of the time. When I was apprentice welding, I felt like the guys didn't like me because I was a girl trying to encroach on their territory. I didn't really feel like I fit in anywhere. My sister and her family were the only break I had from myself. They had friends in their country neighborhood, but their get-togethers mostly involved getting drunk. I didn't really like drinking that much, but when I was around it and when I got started, I was just like them, not knowing when to quit. I felt guilty for drinking in front of her kids. I didn't think it was a very good example to be setting.

My sleeping patterns weren't very good either. I went through cycles of restlessness for two or three nights in a row. After the third night I would be so tired that I'd finally pass out and get a couple nights of rest. But I was always a restless sleeper. I'd wake up with the blankets completely wrapped around me at times from all the movement in my sleep. I never remembered my dreams either. It had been years since I could remember dreaming anything at night. Once in a blue moon, I would remember one and when I did it seemed quite significant.

Stress wasn't easy for me to handle. I had done well as a Tilesetter. I had great contracts through a reliable company and I was starting to get my own private contracts, as well. I was good at what I did. I had the patience for detailed work and I had the design skills to go along with it. It was the stress of having my own company that made me restless and sick. It kept me up at night when I should have been sleeping soundly.

It was also during these seven years that I focused a lot on music and playing the guitar. I wrote numerous songs and spent a lot of time playing in the evenings and on weekends. It wasn't until my last year in my little home that I had someone to play with though. An old friend of mine from my tree planting days, and a fellow hippie-like soul was working not too far from where I was living. We would get together once or twice a week and practice. We even wrote a few songs together.

I had one girlfriend while I was out there. We were together in secret for almost three years. I thought she was the love of my life and I would have loved to have grown old with her at the time. To make a long story short, she broke my heart. That was all I could handle, losing Fen took me a couple years or more to get over and I was never the same after that. I was just surviving, that's all I could do. I needed to go home; I was done with the Wild West. I wanted to be closer to my mother.

I had gone out to Alberta, a feisty and fiery gal ready to take on the world. I went back home a wee bit tamer

Saying goodbye to Christine and her family was the hardest part of the journey back. Mom was happy to have me move back. I was happy to be back. I stayed with my Grandmother when I first arrived in Ontario. Oh how I'd missed all the lakes and the massive amounts of spruce trees.

I thought everything was going to be okay now, I didn't feel so alone. I didn't care that I was making half the money I could have been making out west, this was more important to me. This is where I wanted to be.

I met Sarah a year later.

Sarah and I moved in with each other way too fast in hindsight after only knowing each other for two months, the old lesbian U-Haul syndrome. We needed each other though.

Sarah is the one who suggested I see my nurse about getting some depression pills. I was against it at first, not liking the idea of taking pharmaceuticals, but during a severe bout of depression, I thought Sarah was right, I needed help. That's when I started taking 10mgs of Cipralex, the very same pills I stopped taking at Diamond's when I arrived on this trip.

But, let's get back to the present time, here on the highway in the Greyhound bus.

I looked out the front of the window to see the yellow painted lines on the pavement just ahead swerve gradually over to the left. The bus was weaving over the road, jerking me back to the now. I sat up, alert and realized that the bus driver was falling asleep. I called out to him, "getting tired?"

He kind of wriggled in his seat and answered, "yeah."

"Okay, then," I was trying to think of something to talk to him about that would keep him awake for the rest of the ride.

"It's the last 20 minutes of the ride," he told me, "it seems to be the hardest for me." I looked up ahead to see the sprawling lights of the city in our reach. It reminded me of a story.

"There she is, Grande Prairie, the city where I had my one and only broken heart. Her name was Fen Walker, and she was the cutest little thing I had ever seen. I'm tellin' ya she cast a spell on me! She took my breath away. I thought I was going to marry that girl and grow old with her."

He was curious, "what happened?"

"Well, everything was there between us; we had all the pieces of the pie, but the relationship was fiery and Fen wanted it kept in the closet for too long. I was out to my family and friends and she had never had a girlfriend before. Truth is, I don't think she was gay; she just fell for me for some reason. But after spending more than one Christmas at my sister's alone while she celebrated with her family, I had come to realize that we would be nothing more than a secret affair. That was no way to live a life. Our relationship stood still because it had nowhere to grow in a closet. It tore me to pieces until the day I realized it was over, and it hadn't even had the chance to truly begin. I have never felt what I had for her before, and I haven't since. My sister told me I should write a song to say goodbye to her. And I did. It's called, 'So long, farewell.'"

"Do you guys keep in touch?" he asked.

"No, not really, she stopped having time for me when she opened up her own bakery while we were still seeing each other. But, we left it on a good note and all. The last time I heard from her she wished me a happy birthday last summer through email. She got pregnant by some guy and had a baby. He's living with her now. He's some oilfield worker guy. Guess she could tell her folks about him!"

He looked at me with a surprised kind of smile on his face. "You just bare all, eh?" I gather he wasn't used to a complete stranger talking with him on such an intimate level upon a first meeting. But I didn't care at this point. (In case you didn't already know, I have been becoming manic)

"Well, why not? I'll probably never see you again after this anyway. So, really, I have nothing to lose." It's true, why be guarded when you can open up without fear of being judged by a stranger. What did I care what he thought of me? Besides, I was totally entertaining him and I liked being able to share my stories.

Mission accomplished, Grande Prairie loomed before us and we were headed in. I had successfully kept the bus driver awake and more alert than he had been. Perhaps that is why the only seat that was available on the bus when I got on was this one. Anyone else sitting here would probably have been passed out in slumberville like most of the other riders. My life felt truly touched.

When we pulled into the bus station and parked in the loading garage, the driver made an announcement to all us patrons that we had to exit the bus even if we were travelling on to Beaverlodge. I guess they have to do a mandatory search at main depots, I don't know. All I knew is that I was staying on this bus to head on to Beaverlodge, but for now I had to get off.

"Passengers can reload in 20 minutes" the driver called out. I still didn't know his name. It didn't matter anyway.

The territory was very familiar to step into as I got off the bus. I have been here many times in the past. Walking ahead, I passed through the doors that entered into the waiting area of the station, also the ticket purchasing area. It was fairly crowded here, but still had breathing room. It was a very big place, sitting only less than 60 people in its dated orange cushion chairs with silver arm rests. I had a glow on, a 4 days lack of sleep manic glow. I'm pretty sure I had a little smile on my face or at least a sparkle in my eye at this early morning hour. The sun would be waking up soon, which is more than I can say for the patrons of the station at this time. Most people looked tired and non-communicative. Here we were, stuck in a station together with nothing to say. We just look down, or around and stick to ourselves. What are we hiding from each other, other than ourselves? What are we afraid of?

The door to the buses opened half way, and a uniformed man stuck his head into the room. In a low, heavily accented voice he said "Edmuntonne." I looked around at the standing people and saw that nobody really noticed him. "Ed-mun-tonne," he said again, and stayed to look for a few seconds, then shuffled back behind the door he held open. It closed behind him.

I knew nobody heard him, or even knew he had been standing there. He barely said it loud enough for me to hear and I was standing only a few feet away. I had to do something.

I stood tall and asked aloud in a powerful voice, "Is anyone going to Edmonton?" Five people looked over and started moving through to the loading side. I saved them from missing their bus. What would they have done? I suppose they would have waited for the next one, but their luggage was already loaded, or was it? Nobody said thank you as they walked through the doors behind me, but they probably didn't realize what I had done for them. I felt good, regardless. I knew.

Watching the clock throughout my wait I made sure to be back to the bus five minutes early. Punctuality wasn't something I am normally known for, but at this moment I was proud to be the first one in line. The bus driver smiled at me. He was standing next to an older man with clean cut and nicely brushed white hair who was wearing the same uniform as him.

"Good timing," he said, as he let me on the bus with a wink. I smiled and climbed the stairs up to my seat. I sat and watched as all the other passengers single filed up the stairs and passed me.

As it turns out, the white haired man was taking over the driving duties from here. He climbed up the stairs as he was still in a conversation with the previous driver. "That's rare," he said, "on a Saturday night, that's rare." He sat down in the driver's seat and the original driver stood on the first platform step of the bus just beneath me. I had a feeling they were talking about me and how I had helped him to stay awake for the last little bit of the drive. They exchanged a little bit of shop talk for a minute and then it was time for us to take off. The first bus driver wished the new driver a good trip and said goodbye. Before he stepped off the bus, he looked at me and said goodbye to me as well.

"Nice meeting you," I said.

He smiled, "nice to meet you, take care." With that, he was gone.

The sun was on the rise, and a new day had begun.

This driver was clearly a veteran of the job. He had done it all and seen it all within the bus lines. As we were driving through the city of Grande Prairie, in all its familiarity, I couldn't help but be curious as to what it's like to be a bus driver for a company like Greyhound. I was still wondering what I was going to do for a job now that I had quit tree planting.

I asked him, "So, how do you become a driver for Greyhound anyway?"

"Are you thinking of becoming a driver?" He asked.

"I'm not sure, I was just curious about it."

He was happy to give me a rundown of details about how to apply. His manner was formal, yet warm. I got the impression he liked to teach people about what he knew.

He informed me that the head office was in Edmonton, and that is where you apply. It's not easy to get a job with Greyhound; there are a lot of applicants.

"They look at your driver's abstract to see if you've been in any accidents." He continued.

"Oh, well, I just recently got ticketed for failure to yield." I told him about what happened, that a driver coming towards me had their signal light on and I thought they were turning into where I was pulling out from. They didn't. Apparently they had just pulled out onto the street a little further up and their signal light hadn't turned off yet. I pulled out, they struck me.

The driver nodded his head and said "yes" as though he had heard it all before. He knew never to trust a signal light and to wait until the vehicle had shown you with your own eyes that it was turning before pulling out. I knew now too, I learnt it the hard way.

He shared some more accident stories with me, not his own, but ones that he had been told about over the years. Being a professional driver, I'm sure he has a lot of crash tales.

"And, I've had a few speeding tickets, but I've definitely learned my lesson."

"Well, that might be okay still. How old are you?" He asked.

"Thirty-five," I replied.

"Because they like mature driver's but after the age of Thirty-five they question whether the person can be properly trained or not. They like people to be trained to drive the way they want them to and they figure too many bad habits could be formed that are irreversible by a certain age." I had a couple strikes against me in an already large pile of applicants. It would be a cool job though; I'd get to see a lot of the countryside.

"You never know though, it's worth a shot. Look up the Greyhound website and find out where exactly to send your resume." He was very positive and helpful.

We chit-chatted through the sunrise, well, I listened to him tell more stories. He was a very informative man, one who commanded respect and one's best behaviour. It was different talking to him than it was to the first driver. The first driver was more my age and much less formal. This man was like a father-figure type; he took command of the conversation and allowed me to listen to his stories. The time passed quickly on our 40 minute drive to Beaverlodge.

Then there she was, the little 2100 population town I had lived in for almost 7 years. We passed the largest Beaver in the world that sits as a welcome to the town just off the highway where many tourists stop to get their picture taken. I smiled when I saw it again.

The bus parked in front of the local Arctic Cat retail shop to let me off. I was the only one getting off here; the others must have been travelling on to Dawson Creek or further. The Driver got out before me and opened up the baggage compartment under the bus. My bags were already organized to get off here, so he knew which ones were mine. After he lifted my second duffel bag out from underneath the bus he placed it beside my first one on the ground. He closed the compartment door, turned to me and wished me luck, and then proceeded to get back on the bus, closed the door and drove away.

I was left in the early morning light with my bags, violin and the quietness of the sleepy town. I moved my bags to sit up next to the building out of the way and texted my sister to let her know I had arrived and where the bus had dropped me off. She was on her way to town and would be here in about 10-15 minutes. I was excited to see them, but couldn't stand still to wait. I hadn't been in this town for a couple of years now and I wanted to go and see my house. It wasn't far; I could be back before Christine got here. I left my bags there and simply carried my violin with me. It didn't seem like a single soul was around anyway.

Chapter Eight – The Reunion

As I was walking past the little downtown it felt to me like Beaverlodge had gotten cleaner somehow. It was like the whole town had a paint job to make it look brighter. I only had a couple more streets to go before I got to my little "cabin in the town," as I used to call it, when I got a text from Christine.

Christine: Where r u?

ME: Just up the street a little, I'll be right there

Christine: k

There they were. She had brought her two youngest girls with her, Tilly and Kaya. They were standing next to their submarine of an old eighties suburban. When they saw me, the kids screamed "Erin," with glee and ran towards me. I knelt down and greeted them with open arms as they entangled me with theirs. How I loved these children and how they loved me.

"Erin, I missed you," Tilly said to me after we finished our group hug.

"Yeah, Erin, I missed you, too," Kaya chirped into the conversation.

"I missed you guys too, very much and I thought about you every day," and I did, I loved them that much.

I got up to greet my sister, who was waiting with a smile on her face. "Hello," she said in a happy tone. We were both smiling from both the inside and out upon seeing each other. I gave her a hug also.

"Okay my lil' Tilly, how 'bout you hang onto this violin while your mom and I get the rest of this baggage into the back of your truck?"

Tilly loves music as well and has a good ear for it. She gleamed at having the job of looking after her auntie's violin. Christine and I made quick work of putting the bags in the back and we all hopped into the truck.

"Are you hungry? I thought we could go grab some breakfast at the Inn." She suggested.

"Sure, sounds good." I couldn't stop looking at my family; I was so filled with joy to be around them. I looked back into the seats behind me to see two little chipper happy smiling faces beaming back at me. It felt so good to be around people who loved me too.

"We can go by your house on the way. You know, your renters are paranoid!"

I looked at her, not really concerned with the gossip of my renters. I barely kept in contact with them. They just put the money in every month and I didn't bother them and they didn't bother me. It was an arrangement I was quite happy with. "Why do you say that?" I asked her.

"They put up cameras around your place."

"Cameras? Hmm, oh well, I don't care. They can do what they want as long as they pay the rent."

"They don't really look after the yard either; it used to look so much nicer when you were there."

We were driving by my house and I caught a glimpse of it, but I couldn't stop looking at my sister and her kids, I was just so elated to be here with them. So, I barely even saw the house, which was the whole point of driving past it. Oh well, I'll see it later, I thought.

The kids had a bunch of stories they wanted to share with me. The truck was filled with conversation the whole way to the restaurant. I was impressed by how well-spoken her girls were. They had grown in spurts since last I had seen them, obviously.

We pulled into the parking lot of the Beaverlodge Inn and went inside to find a booth. I was proud as a peacock to be walking in with my family. I felt like I was standing six inches taller.

We parked ourselves into a nice window-side booth and checked out the menu. I wasn't even reading it. Christine was asking the girls what they would like, and pointing choices out for them on their kid's menu. I glanced at mine and skimmed over it, but wasn't really seeing it. Eggs and ham and toast and home fries, that's what I was having.

When the waitress came over I noticed this large tattoo on her forearm. The artwork really caught my eye. "Wow, that's one of the nicest tattoos I've seen in awhile," I told her. She seemed pleased with the compliment, as most people do. I wanted to take a better look at it. "Can I see it closer?"

"Sure," she held her arm out closer to me so I could take a look. What caught my eye was the globe; I have one on my left foot with wings. It symbolizes being able to go anywhere and do anything you want. I've had it since I was 18. The waitress' tattoo had the earth with the North American continent and the South American continent painted green. The words "Dusty Storm" were written in the surrounding ocean. Something was breaking out of the top of the Earth; it looked to me like some sort of angel with a Native American twist. The sky was painted ocean blue around the angel with bright yellow stars. I liked it, although I didn't know what it meant. Surprisingly, I didn't ask either.

"Can I take a picture of it? A friend of mine is really into tattoos and I'd like her to see this one."

She didn't mind at all, "Sure," she said and kept her arm out so I could snap it onto my phone.

She took our order, pleasantly, and I watched as Christine's children were coaxed into telling her their own order. Shyness runs in our family. The girls were given a couple of paper place mats to colour and a cup filled with colourful crayons.

I sent the picture to Sarah. She loves tats and this was a cool one. She'd like to fill both of her arms up throughout her life. At this moment she has a half sleeve, and several others scattered over her body. But she wasn't impressed with me taking this shot for some reason. She thought it was odd of me to want to take a picture of the waitress' tattoo. I was starting to feel like I could never make her happy. What was wrong with chatting up a waitress about her tat? I still wanted Sarah to be a part of my journey and sharing random photos of cool stuff I see was a way of doing it. Oh well, I was with my family now and I'm not going to get my feathers all ruffled up over it.

"I'm going to take a picture of you guys now, you all look so cute!"

"OK," the little girls chirped, still at the age where they smile happily at the camera and like to have their picture taken. I got up from the table. I had to back up a little to get both girls and Christine in the shot. Got it!

"Nice boots," an older man said to me from the booth just in front of where we were sitting. Again with the boots, they must have really caught the working class man's eye.

"Thanks, a friend of mine gave them to me." I don't remember now what else he said but he started a conversation with me about something and I went and sat down across from him at his booth for a minute to chat. Turns out he was a trucker, another job I had considered doing. He was sitting alone eating his breakfast, so I asked him to join me and my family at our table for some conversation. He was a plump older man with greying hair underneath his trucker's hat. He accepted my offer to join us, grabbed his plate and took my seat.

Our food had been brought to the table by the time I got back to it, and I moved my plate over to the end of the table and pulled an extra chair over for me to sit on.

He was very sociable, but a little strange. I introduced him to "my sister, Christine, and her two kids, Tilly and Kaya."

"Sisters, eh, who is the older one?" He looked at me and he looked at her.

Christine was being polite with him, "I am," she replied.

"I see," he continued, "and how are you two little girls?" He was looking at Kaya and Tilly.

"Good," they said, a little shy with him.

I wasn't really appetized by my food even though I hadn't really eaten that much in the last day.

The trucker told us his name, but I forgot it almost as soon as he told me. Whatever his name was, he liked asking questions and telling stories.

We told him about how Christine home schools her children, and that she has five of them now. He was interested in what we thought about homeschooling, so we had a discussion on that.

I was interested in his trucker stories and fantasized about what it would be like. Again, my mind was racing into possibilities. I didn't realize until now, through writing this, that my mind was so over-reactive and jumpy from one thing to the next without sustained action to back it up. I now understand mania.

He told us about a man and a woman who trucked together, but weren't lovers. That's when I started to feel uncomfortable around him. The way he was talking to Christine and I and the kids gave me a funny feeling, but I wasn't well. Sometimes I would look at Christine and beam a smile at her while holding her gaze for a long time.

"You see that," the trucker spoke, "that's love right there. She's looking at you with love in her eyes." Christine nodded her head and had a little smile on her lips, but she was thinking something.

I was trying to eat my food, but found that I only stared at it. I was spacing out and then jerked back to where I was. I would look out the window and stare as well. I really needed some sleep; it was caving in on me now. The trucker must have noticed,

"She's in rough shape," he said to Christine. Christine nodded her head and looked a little upset. I didn't realize how bad of shape I looked at that point, but I couldn't hold a train of thought very well and when I tried to eat I would only stare at the food with my fork in my hand. I wasn't hungry.

I didn't really know why Christine was crying at the table, but she had tears running down her cheeks. In the back of my mind I knew, I knew that she was worried about me.

I thought I was doing a lonely trucker a favour by asking him to join us, but when he turned the conversation over to women being sexually abused I knew that I had made a mistake and regretted ever inviting him over in the first place. I told him to stop talking about that, that it wasn't appropriate conversation, especially not in front of these young girls.

He looked at me and fluttered his eyelids in doe-like fashion, "oh, okay, so you want to be naïve." I didn't appreciate his comment. I wanted him to leave. He kept talking about something, but at this point all that was running through my head was that I was exhausted.

"Listen, mister, I've had enough. I'm sorry, but I just need to be left alone with my family." I was blunt and straight-forward about it. He got the point; I don't see how he couldn't. He left on a polite note. His meal was finished anyway.

Christine told me I should try to eat, but I let her know I wasn't hungry right now. "We'll get it packed up then, you need to go home and sleep." Christine definitely was a mother. I was never safer than I was right now.

I texted Sarah and let her know I was heading out to Christine's place and that the service there was sometimes sketchy.

I don't remember much of the drive to her place. I know from experience that it's a half hour drive out in the country to the area they call Goodfare, but I don't remember any of it; not the conversation we had, nothing. I know I was awake and we were talking, but that's it. Farmer's fields and poplar bush surround us now.

Chapter Nine – Home Away From Home

Christine pulled into her dirt laneway nestled in between poplar bush. It wasn't long for a country laneway, just long enough to be private. It's a minute or two drive up to their house, slowly over the potholes. They no longer lived in the little cabin off of a neighbour's land. Since those days they built this home we were travelling towards. While I was out living here, I helped them at certain phases. I helped them to pour the concrete slab that it rests upon. Lane, Christine's man, is a concrete finisher by trade. I helped them frame. I helped them to put the roofing on. I helped them sand the drywall. Most of the work, however, was done by them. It still wasn't finished, but it was liveable. It was in the same shape now as it had been when I left two years ago.

They don't have much grass. It's all dirt and bush. The house loomed in front of me. It was a giant box-shaped beast finished in stained plywood. The left side was Lane's shop where he did his mechanical work keeping their vehicles on the road. Attached on the right was their living space. All the windows and doors had been salvaged, stripped and repainted.

Lane was outside chopping wood with an old axe. The pile surrounded him on the wet, snow dusted ground. I got out of the truck and a little timidly walked over to him. Lane and I have always had a love-hate relationship.

He took another swing of the axe and split through another piece of wood when he looked up at me. "Oh, Erin," he said under his breath, as though he had to put up with me now.

"Hi Lane," I pretended I didn't hear him and tried to act friendly. I didn't want to fight with him.

Lane was a fighter by nature. He would get into fist fights at the bar when he was younger and his strong mind and opinionated points of view got him into verbal fights as well. He is a dominant character. He also has a charm about him that makes him likeable and interesting to be around. The conversation was rarely dull when he was in the room, at times, however, it was aggravating. He had a childlike, boyish energy about him coupled with a fierce redneck man's will. A beer was never far away as well as a rolled smoke to go with it after the tailor mades were all gone.

Outside a gathering spot for the family was the fire pit. In the warmer months they often cooked their meals fireside style and sat out in the night together. There's a trampoline not far from it and the kids loved to jump on it off and on throughout the day.

The family is pretty proud of their garden; it is huge, about the size of an Olympic swimming pool. My sister has a green thumb and she is passing that down to her children. They have a section that is devoted just for them to take care of. Since I've been gone they have built a greenhouse where they grow a jungle of food. They also now have a bunch of chickens that lay fresh eggs for them every morning. Homesteading is their dream, and they're doing it; their way and at their pace, slowly but surely.

Going into the door of the shop was a little claustrophobic. Christine's old car was in there having some work done on it. Tools, bolts, rags, boots, and things were scattered all over the floor. Years of tools and things were there. There wasn't much floor to walk on. This is how it often was in the shop, Lane's escape pad where he tinkers and sits by the wood stove to listen to the CBC radio with his morning coffee. The shop has seen many visits from many friends sharing a drink and a story. Some of the empty beer cans were still floating around to prove it.

I went through the door to the house quarters and was greeted by a little two year old smiling boy. "Oh, Logan!" I said as I swooped down to pick him up. "What a cutie you are!" The last time I saw him he was just a baby and now here he was a walking little monkey. He wasn't talking yet. He just looked at me with those big brown eyes and smiled. He was simply irresistible. Christine was blessed with five beautiful children. I like to joke that she had enough kids for the both of us. I just wish she didn't live so far away across the country so we could see them more often. Christine and Lane were standing behind me with smiles on their faces as they saw my reaction to their youngest child.

I put Logan down as I walked into the open concept house. It was such a familiar space to be in. I had spent many a day here visiting. It was my second home out west. Nothing was fancy here, everything was simple. The kitchen table was an old used 1950's style with stainless steel legs and four white and orange cushioned chairs to match. Some of the stuffing had been torn loose on the chairs and were in need of repair. The large, 8x10 picture window shone sunlight on a table where Christine had her new budding herbs and tomato plants. The L-shaped kitchen counter and cupboards were salvaged from a neighbor's renovation project. These people were thrifty. They wanted to be and they had to be.

The final stage of completion for the inside was the painted drywall. It had yet to be trimmed. The electrical had been run through the house but not hooked up. They have a propane stove, a cooler for a fridge, a wood stove for heat, a pump well for water and a generator for electricity. They run power cords into the house off of it and use bar cords for extra outlets. That's how they watch cableless T.V., movies, run video games and plug in lamps and fish tanks. There's always something alive to grow and take care of in this house.

It was a constant battle for my sister to keep it clean. There was always a pile of dishes to do and a pile of clothes to go with it. Christine had to take her laundry into town to wash it at the laundromat. I'm sure a washer and dryer is one of the only things she misses from today's modern day living. When she takes a load into town it's never a light one. She's the woman with five garbage bags full of clothes to do; all clothes that had been bought at a thrift store and handed down to her from her neighbors.

I was glad to be here. This feels like home. Whatever tiredness I felt at the restaurant was now long gone and I was all riled up and cheerful to be amongst my sister and her family.

Coming down the stairs on the left side of the living room was Jacob, Christine's eldest. He was now walking towards me with a darling smile on his lips.

"Oh my God!" I said as he approached me. He kept smiling as he came nearer. "You have grown so much Jacob!" I told him as I walked over to him to give him a hug. He was tall and skinny like his father. He was only about to turn 14 years old but he was taller than me and I'm 5'8. If this was his awkward years then the girls better watch out when he starts driving and gets a car. Jacob is a sweet boy. He has a lot of the same interests as his father, cars, quads, snowmobiles, dirt bikes. He promised to show me his used bike that he got not long ago. Awesome, I thought, I liked bikes too. The last time I was here I helped Jacob strip down and repaint his bicycle, now he was riding dirt bikes.

Then I saw Gracie, one of the artists of the family. I gave her a big hug too. Christine has her drawings and pictures hung up around the house. Gracie love's art and science. She conducts her own experiments at home as well. She told me of attempting to set up the right environment for hatching Chinese fighting fish. Of course, we all probably think our kids are talented, but maybe that's because they are. Our true selves are never more real than when they are shown to us in their childhood before the weight of the world starts to wear on their shoulders.

I think everyone was pretty excited that I was there, maybe even Lane, although he would never admit to it.

I looked on the table and saw a large decanter filled with red wine. "Jordan's sister made that and gave it to us," Christine told me. Jordan was a friend and neighbor of theirs. They had known each other for years through ups and downs. "You want a glass? Maybe it will help you sleep."

"She needs some whiskey or something hard," Lane said. But they didn't have any of that stuff anyway.

"I don't know," I thought.

"Go on, have a glass, it'll help." Christine must have filled Lane in about my lack of sleep. This would be the beginning of day 5 without it. I had never had this happen to me before. It was like I was on a high.

"Alright then," I took a glass of wine and had a sip. "Mmm, that's pretty good."

"Yeah, she made it from her own grapes and everything," Christine told me. One thing homesteader types are proud of is their ability to do things themselves and I don't blame them.

"Let me look at your hair," Christine was trying to see the back of my head. Before I came out west I had my hair cut, well shaved, in the back. I still had bangs and longer, jagged hair coming down the sides of my face. If you saw me from the front you wouldn't be able to tell right away that the back of my head was shaved.

Christine looked it over closely while contemplating on whether or not she liked it. "Did you do that yourself?" It was a legitimate question seeing as when I lived out here I did cut my own hair. I hadn't been to an actual hair salon for years. I even cut Christine's hair once, and I think since then she started to cut her own.

 "No, I had it done, what do you think? It's a party in the front, business in the back! Get it?" I was smiling, "it's the opposite!"

Christine laughed, "I don't know yet if I like it or not." I appreciated her honesty. It didn't matter if she liked it or not anyway, it was done and I kind of enjoyed it. It was different to feel the back of your head when it was bristly, and I no longer had to worry about bed head.

"Hey Erin, want to see a card trick?" Gracie had come over to me with a stack of cards in her hand.

"Sure, I love card tricks." I told her.

"Okay," she fanned the cards out in front of her and asked me to pick one.

I looked at them and teasingly acted as though I didn't know which one to pick. I ran my finger along the back of them and said "hmm" as I pondered my decision. "I'll pick this one," I said as I peeled a card out from the middle.

"That one, okay" Gracie was looking forward to dazzling me with her magic. I was already impressed by the thought alone of being shown a card trick. I liked this kind of stuff. I taught myself to juggle when I was Gracie's age. One day I saw a juggling clown on TV and I decided I wanted to be able to do that. So I got three tennis balls and kept trying all afternoon until I finally taught myself how. I couldn't wait to show my mother what I had learned. Maybe that's how Gracie was feeling right now.

She folded the fanned cards back into a pile and cut the deck. I was holding a three of hearts in my hand, which I kept securely hidden from her. She shuffled the pile a little awkwardly and then fanned the deck out again. "Now, place the card back in the deck anywhere," were my next instructions. I placed it more towards the middle. Again, she closed the fan, split the deck and did a little shuffle. She tapped the top of the deck, split the pile again, and tapped it for a second time.

"Is this your card?" she asked me as her thumb pushed the top card of the deck towards me. I picked it up and looked at it.

I was impressed and let out a little snort of air, "Why yes, Gracie, it is! Wow, that's really impressive." I smiled at her and tousled the top of her dirty blond coloured head in approval. She tilted her head to the side with a modest smile and her blue eyes beamed.

Christine was standing behind the counter beside us and exclaimed that she now knew how that trick worked. Gracie must have done it to her before. "They're all three of hearts!" She boasted with the pride of finally figuring it out.

"Mah-OM!" Gracie was disappointed by having her magic be turned to dust.

"Oh, yeah!" I liked having the trick revealed, "lemme see the deck."

Gracie handed it to me and sure enough they were all three of hearts. She didn't have a full 52 card deck of them yet, but enough to fool you. The backs were all the same, so one would just assume they are different cards and suits. "Good one!" I told her. "You fooled me."

Chapter Ten – Running On Empty

It was always very active in Christine's house, children playing, people talking and going in and out of the house. Somebody always wanted to show you something, or tell you something, or do something with you.

I gave my packed up breakfast meal to Jacob, he was hungry like a growing boy always is, so I let him enjoy it. I sat at the table with Jacob while he ate and sipped my wine.

Little Logan came walking over to me, arms held out a little for balance and gave me one of his little toy trucks. He tried to tell me what it was, "Tr-uh, Tr- uh", but the little sweetie couldn't quite pronounce it.

"Thank you Logan, it's a really cool Ter-uh-kkk," I emphasized to him. "Ter-uh-kkk," I said a few more times, but his k's weren't going to sound out this very moment, he needed more time for them to develop. It's pretty charming when kids are just starting to talk. What an amazing accomplishment that is for us humans.

I couldn't help but to pick him up and hug him. He sat on my knee at the table while we played with his trucks, driving and crashing and touring around, even on the roads in the sky. The cheerful cries of laughter children release are contagious.

~

Lane was out in the shop sitting in his chair by the stove drinking his coffee and rolling his Drum tobacco into a tiny spliff. I joined him with my glass of wine. For all of the argumentative banter that had gone on between Lane and I over the years, I still wanted to spend time with him. I was always a little guarded when I was around him though because I never knew when an argument would rear its ugly face.

CBC radio was on and played nice and clear through the wired up old style speakers they had picked up somewhere, maybe they were out of an old car, I never thought to ask. But they were hung up on the wall and able to bellow if a dance party were ever to transpire.

I sat down in one of the cushioned metal legged chairs that were placed around the wood stove amongst the remains of beer cans and mechanical debris. I was unusually excitable and hyper as I looked over beside me to see Lane's project of Christine's old maroon four-door Honda. They had gotten this car when I was still living out west. I remember the day Lane brought it home from Edmonton after buying it off of his brother. I was visiting with Christine at the time. But when I look at it now sitting there it's like I appreciated it for the first time. It was just a regular old car. There was nothing special about it but I really started to admire it. I got up from my chair and stood in front of it, smoking in the lit rolled tobacco spliff that Lane had offered me.

"Whooeee, she's a beauty," I was in awe. I wasn't feeling shy around Lane at all either, which I normally was around him, or at least more reserved. But not at this moment. At this moment I was like a little tom-boy wanting to hang out with the boys in the shop and drool over the project at hand. I was looking at it like it was an old 1970's mustang sitting there in need of a few touch ups. I looked it all over, the lines, the interior, under the hood. I don't think Lane knew quite what to make of me at the moment; it was the first time I had acted like this around him.

Jacob was out in the shop with us. He had a tube of silicone and hopped up on the top of the car, laid down and started to silicone the top of the front window. "Jacob, don't," his dad wanted him to stop. I think Jacob was trying to impress me with his skills. He has learnt a lot about mechanics from his Dad over the years. I thought it was real sweet.

Christine came out and sat with us after I was done drooling over the car. While we were talking the door to the living quarters opened and little Tilly and Kaya came through with piles of paper in their hands. They walked over to me and showed me what was on them. They were all filled with drawings they had worked on for me. Tilly had her own pile, as well as Kaya had hers. Some of them were activity drawings they wanted me to complete. On one page, Tilly had made a row of different styled dresses. Under that row was a line of different styled shoes, under it a line of different styled necklaces and finally a row of differently styled hair. Tilly wanted me to circle my favourite in each row. They must have been preparing for my visit. It made me feel very special, just as I wanted them to feel. I sat and looked at every picture both of them had drawn up, and took the time to do every activity page they had come up with. Christine and Lane watched on as I interacted with their children, they could always see how much I cared for them.

~

Later that morning Christine had to go and milk a cow at Gary Shmitt's farm. He was a neighbour of theirs who had an arrangement with them that if they milked the cow, they got paid in it. That's how they always had fresh milk to drink. So she and I and the two youngest girls went for the ride with her.

On the way I told her a little about Sarah and I's arguments. I said I wasn't sure what to do. I didn't know if I should keep trying to work it out, or if we were just too opposite to jive, even though we had so much in common at the same time. I asked Christine's opinion but she said she couldn't know because she doesn't know Sarah. When I was seeing Fen, Christine was with me throughout that whole relationship.

She was right there listening through it all like a soap opera was being told to her week to week. This time, however, she's not around me to know the details and I missed her advice.

We pulled into Gary's long laneway and drove on up to the house. Across the land to the west side I could see my old green 1989 Ford pick-up truck. Gary had bought it off me to use as a water truck when I moved back home.

"There she is," I said out loud. "I loved that old truck. She was pretty sexy in her old age."

"Something's wrong with it, it's been sitting for a bit," Christine told me.

"What's up with it?"

"Don't think he knows. He wants Lane to come over and take a look at it."

"Well I'm going to walk over there and say hello to it while you're milking the cow."

"Alright."

"You little monkeys want to come with me to say hello to my old green beast?"

"Yes!" Both Tilly and Kaya chirped excitedly. Off we went.

We had to walk past a herd of cows to get to the truck. Gary had electric wire fences set up to keep the cows where he wanted them, and shelters along the way. We stopped to take a good look at them as we were walking by through the pasture. I told the girls that their mom and I grew up around cows and that we'd rip out the tall grass around our fence line and feed it to their slobbering mouths. I told them how the cow's long pointy tongue would curl around the grass and pull it back right from our hands and then chew with their mouths open. We laughed.

There was a girl with long dark hair dressed in blue overalls carrying a bucket of food around in by the shelter for the cows. I noticed her for the first time and greeted her with a hello. She had a thick accent that I recognized as being French. She was polite and friendly, yet kept busy with chores. Gary's farm is a WWOOFing farm. He is part of the World Wide Opportunities for Organic Farms organization. He has had many travelling visitors stay with him to learn about organic farming from all over the world.

"We're just headed over to take a look at that truck," I pointed over to the green beast. "I owned it before Gary."

"Ah," she smiled.

I wasn't sure how much of the language she understood. The girls and I carried on to our original destination.

Tilly and Kaya were running and exploring ahead of me. They were comfortable at Gary's farm; they had been here many times before.

When I got up close to my old girl I ran my hand down the side of her smooth green curved shape by the hood. She had gotten pretty banged up on the farm. There were fresh dents along both her sides. Guess she was earning her keep. On her extended cab box there were two gas tanks. The first one had the word "gas" written on the cover, the second one had "no gas" written on it. The back tank has a leak in it from being rusted out. I can imagine Gary having to remind the WWOOFers to not put gas in the second tank all the time until he finally just wrote on the covers.

Somebody had taken my bumper sticker off, "If ya ain't gonna pass, get off my ass."

Well now, I thought, what could be the trouble with you my old girl? I only had a problem with her once while I was driving her. It was when I was all packed up with my stuff in the back of it and ready to take the final drive out to Christine's with a load of my belongings when it wouldn't start in my driveway at my little house in Beaverlodge. My renter, Kelvin, figured out the problem for me. He went to a scrap yard and found a replacement plug of some kind for me and installed it, free of charge.

I went to open the hood, but someone had tied it shut with metal wire and it was tight. I tried to release it with just my hands, but couldn't budge it, I could barely get my fingers in close enough to try and get at it. I needed some wire cutters. At this point in time I felt like I could fix it. I wasn't a mechanic, but I thought I could somehow figure it out. How hard could it be? Part of being manic for me at that time was that I didn't see things as being too difficult. I thought that at the basis of it all, everything was simple. If I could look under the hood I figured a simple solution would be waiting for me to figure it out. I knew the battery was dead, that would be a start.

"Come on girls, let's go to the mechanic shop over there for a sec."

We headed to the mechanic quarters of the farm. It wasn't far from where the truck was parked tucked in by some background trees. There was a little shed filled with tires and odds and ends that may or may not be used for scrap parts. Most of it was probably just junk. The larger shop was just beyond it. It had a cement floor and a workbench that was more organized. The girls and I snooped. I was snooping for wire cutters, the girls were just snooping for curiosity's sake.

I liked this shop. I liked feeling like I was on a mission to help Gary fix my old truck. I liked having a puzzle to figure out. A piece was missing that I had to find and the first step was to get those wire cutters in my hands, which I found, quite easily, sitting on the wooden bench.

The girls were exploring the shop. There was a loft of some kind at the back of it. I walked around the west side of the building towards an open doorway that led to some stairs.

"Let's go check out up stairs, guys."

"Ok," they were game.

I fumbled around looking for the light switch. My mind felt like it was on a mission just to find the light switch, like everything was a test of my intelligence. I found it, and I passed another test.

We climbed the stairs and found a homey loft at the top of them that was decked out with its own kitchen. It was only about 100 sq ft, but it was appealing with a bed on the right hand side and a little living space beyond it where you could cook and look out onto the farm from a double sided window. I wondered how many WWOOFers had stayed here before. Again, my mind was imagining a plan. I could be the resident mechanic on the farm while staying in this loft. Sarah and I could stay here together.

We went back down the stairs and wandered out of the shop slowly. I had the wire cutters still in my   hand.

We walked back over to the truck. I cut the wire and opened the hood up. I started to check things over, looking for cracks in hoses, seeing if all the fluids were up. The water tank was empty. I thought that was ironic, the water tank of the water truck was empty. Really, I had no idea what I was looking for, I had never fixed a vehicle in my life, but in my mind I felt like I was in some kind of a genius state. I'm not saying I think I'm a genius. I think a part of being manic makes you feel like you are, I don't understand it, I just know what I felt. I was so overly confident in my lack of skill with mechanics that I thought Gary would want me to stay and be his mechanic. Like that was even a possibility that he needed a full time mechanic around. In reality, he had Lane as a neighbor who worked things out for him when he needed help on machinery. Lane knew what he was doing, I didn't. But, my mind thought I could. It was all a big lie my brain was playing on me.

In the meantime, Gary had pulled into his yard with a trailer on the back of his truck. He had two different laneways, the one Christine pulled into by the house, and this one that led to me. He parked in front of the mechanic shop. The girls ran over to greet him. I thought I should go over there and say hi too seeing as I was on his property and had my nose stuck under the hood of his truck.

Gary knew who I was, he had known of me when I was living out here. To him I would be Christine's little sister, seeing as he knew her and Lane and her family more closely. They went to a lot of the same gatherings and get-togethers; ice fishing on family day, New Year's party at his ranch and so on.

He was still sitting in his truck when I sauntered up to him and he greeted me with a smile. Gary is a kind man who does a lot for his neighbors.

"Hi Gary!"

"Well hello Erin, long time no see."

"Yeah, I just got to Christine's place today. She came out here to milk the cow so I thought I'd take a look at my old truck. I hear you have a problem with it."

"So, what have you got figured out?" He asked. Gary is a patient man that likes to see people learn.

"Well, for starters, the battery is dead."

"Okay, well I think I have an extra one over here in this shed." Gary got out of his truck and all of us walked over to see if we could find it.

I told Gary a little about my trip out here, how I was stranded on the side of the road and hadn't slept for a few days. I was talking very openly with him as well. This is something else that was a little unusual for me because I don't usually disclose personal details of my life to people, I usually keep too much to myself. Gary understood about being overly tired though, he had just returned from a trip to Edmonton to drop off some of his pigs at the farmer's market there. He had been travelling all night without sleep as well. I could see he was a little red-eyed.

We searched around the shed for a minute and Gary had found the battery. I picked it up to carry it over. It was heavy, it felt like 50 lbs.

"Come bring it over to the trailer" Gary said. "It's too heavy to carry all the way over there." He was right, so I brought it over. Gary slid open the door to the big steel livestock trailer. In it there was still a black rubber water bowl and some scattered straw. Gary placed the battery just beyond the door track.

"I want in," Tilly exclaimed.

"You do, okay then." I lifted Tilly up and placed her in the trailer even though she was plenty big enough to get in herself. She stood there with a smile. "Tilly, do you trust Kaya?" I pointed to Kaya.

"Yes," she answered.

"Do you trust me?" I asked while pointing to my chest.

"Yes," she answered.

"Do you trust Gary?" I asked while pointing to Gary.

"Yes," she answered.

"Okay then," I said and I pulled the metal door shut and Tilly was in the dark trailer by herself.

She was only in there a second before she got scared and screamed "let me out, let me out."

I was asking her if she trusted us because I felt like I was preparing her to trust her instincts so that if she ever found herself hitchhiking on the side of the road she would be able to keep herself safe. This was like a mock trial for me. I felt like I was the mother of these two and we were out getting picked up on the side of the road by a stranger and we were going to get a ride in the back of his trailer.

I opened the door as soon as I heard her yell to get out. I didn't want her to be scared. I just wanted her to learn to trust her own instincts because I wouldn't always be there to protect her. She trusted me to know that if she got scared I would open the door.

"I'm going to pull the truck over there." Gary said.

"Do you guys want to go for a ride in the trailer with me?" I asked the girls.

They were excited "Okay!" We hopped in the back and Gary shut the door. At first we all went in and crouched down at the very front of it and prepared ourselves for the ride. Then the playful side of me came out and I got up and did a dance for them while we travelled slowly, but bumpily over to the green beast. The kids laughed with me as I put on my silly show for them pretending to be an exuberant tap dancer. I always did love to entertain Christine's kids in goofy ways, and they loved it too. This was not abnormal for me to do.

We got out of the trailer all smiles and Gary started to take the old battery out of the truck. He made the ole' switcheroo. It didn't make a difference though. I told Gary about the radio, how it had to be turned off in a very specific way. It was wired up directly to the battery and I didn't know if anyone ever told him that a certain button had to be pressed a certain way in order for it to be powered down. I also said the water tank was empty. I'm not sure how Gary was taking this information. I thought I was being helpful and informative but it's probably all stuff he already knew.

"Well, that's all I'm going to do for now with it," Gary said.

"Do you need any help with anything else?" I asked. "I can help with something."

"How about you go and castrate all those cows?" I'm pretty sure he was being sarcastic but I didn't see it at the time. I didn't realize that Gary had had enough for the moment. He was tired and needed to go in and crash. I looked at him to see if he was serious. "I have to get some rest right now, it's been a long night."

"Okay, well I can come back when you're ready for help then," I was very eager. I had never been so eager to help Gary before. I was hardly ever out here except maybe twice, once for a campfire get-together, and once when Christine came out to milk a cow. So by me being so eager to do something on the farm was overdrive. If Gary had wanted to castrate those cows right then and there I would have been game. In some sort of distant dream in the back of my mind I thought I was showing him how much of a help around here I could be and that he would want me to stay and live in the mechanic quarters for food and lodging. He was done, though, and started walking over toward the house. He let me know that he would call me if he needed help.

Christine must have been done milking the cow because she was walking over towards us. She and Gary exchanged a few words in passing.

When she caught up to us I told her I wanted to go and look at the old Ferris wheel. Gary had one on his property and years ago it actually worked and people would take rides on it. Now, however, it sat there like a crippled statue wasting away. We walked over where it sat about half a kilometer away near the front fence of the farm. I climbed up the wooden bench seats that no longer swung to the top and sat there looking over the whole farmland. I imagined Sarah and I playing around these parts, tinkering on fixing the Ferris wheel benches and making them look shiny and new while running around chasing each other through the fields. We could explore our love here, out on a farm in the middle of nowhere in northern Alberta. My excitement rose with the idea, yet another idea.

I climbed back down. The kids were at the bottom of the Ferris wheel copycatting me by sitting on the bottom bench chair that was closest to the ground. We walked back over towards the mechanic shop barn. That's when I noticed another little shed beside it. On the wall of the old wooden barn board was a beautiful picture of an angel. It was a worn down painting. I told Christine I wanted to come back with my camera so I could take a picture of this, it was that unique and breathtaking to me at the time.

On the way home I was relaying to Christine my thoughts on Sarah coming out here to join me for the summer, to stay on Gary's farm as a WWOOFer.

"Why don't you guys go on a real holiday with each other? Why would she want to stay there?" Of course, she was right. Sarah would never have gone for it anyway.

I didn't realize that my mind wasn't linking everything together properly. On one hand I was wondering if Sarah and I could last because we fight a lot, and a few moments later I dreamed up this beautiful love story of us traipsing around a farm together. My mind was working from moment to moment without a tie between them. My memory wasn't linking events together to make my thoughts more realistic and grounding. It was thinking in a very spur of the moment way.

Chapter Eleven - Surfacing

That night after supper and further visiting with the family I finally went to bed. Whenever I slept over at Christine's house I would climb in with her two youngest girls and have a sleepover with them. They would pick out a couple books they'd like me to read as a bedtime story and I would read them in funny voices and ad-libbed lines. They laughed and told me that wasn't part of the story when I made it sound too ridiculous and absurd. Tonight was no different. We shared some stories and then lay there talking until I finally said it's time to go to sleep.

Something I'd never experienced before happened that night. Something I wasn't even aware was possible.

I was dreaming of big bright snakes slithering around. They weren't scary; it was more absurd than scary. The dream went on in the background while Tilly and I were talking to each other. She was influencing my dream in the middle of the night. I don't know whether she was dreaming or not or simply talking with me. I'm known to talk in my sleep. Perhaps I was sleep talking and Tilly started talking back to me. I'm not sure, but I think we were sharing a dream. I was having a semi-conscious conversation with her while it was influencing my dream.

"Erin, there's a snake that lives under my bed," she explained to me matter of factly. She described what it looked like. I played along with her, at this point becoming more and more aware of our conversation. I was talked out of my sleep and now realized what had just happened. I thought it was an amazing experience. It felt like such a surge of shared creativity between two separate human beings.

Tilly and I laid there and shared stories some more, this time while we were completely awake. She told me about the snake under her bed and other animals in her room. When she was done telling me her story she asked me to tell her one. I often made up stories for the kids on the spot as I went along. She wanted me to do that again for her now.

So I thought for a second and began telling her a slightly sad story of a woman who lived in the woods alone without any family. She never cut her hair so it was so long that it dragged behind her like the train of a wedding dress. Tilly listened to my tale told in a faraway slow spoken voice for more effect. I loved that I could let this side out around Christine's kids and that they enjoyed it as well.

"Now it's your turn to tell me a story. Tilly"

"Um, okay, um," her wheels were turning.

I smiled to myself as she began speaking in a raspy scary voice and intensely told me a story that was influenced by the story I had just told her. My heart grew warm listening to her.

~

Sleep was elusive yet again. It was 8 am in the morning now. Tilly was fast asleep. I decided to get up and call Sarah. I was impulsive in my phone calls to Sarah, not really thinking that she might be sleeping. Well, I knew she might be but the overwhelming urge to speak with her over-ruled the compassion to let her stay sleeping. Self-centeredness may be another problem in manic states.

I slowly pulled the blankets off myself, grabbed for my phone on the nightstand and tried to sneak out of the room.

"Erin, where are you going?" I was caught. Tilly had been stirred awake.

"I'm just going downstairs to phone Sarah, you should go back to sleep, sweetie."

"No, Erin, I want to come with you."

"Aren't you tired, Hun?"

"No, I want to go with you." Tilly was my shadow and wanted to always stay by my side while I was there. I didn't mind one bit.

"Okay, well we have to be quiet and not wake anyone else up, okay?"

"Okay," her voice was soft and light.

I held her hand as we walked out of her bedroom and into the hallway that led to the stairs. We walked down the wooden framed steps slowly so as to not make a sound. When we got to the bottom we sat down on one of the living room couches and I called Sarah. Tilly was nestled in next to me with her knees pulled up, still a little sleepy. She yawned a couple of times.

Sarah's voice was quiet, "Hello?"

"Hey," I was trying to talk gently and lowly so as not to disturb my family upstairs. "Sorry if I woke you up but I just really wanted to talk to you."

"It's okay." Ever since I got off the plane and landed out west I had called Sarah at odd hours of the night. "What's up?"

"Well I wanted to tell you about Gary Shmitt's organic farm we went to yesterday." I felt like I had some good stories to relay to her and I couldn't wait any longer. She listened as I told her all about the cow Christine milks and how they bring some home for themselves; I told her about the WWOOFer from France and a little about the program. I told her that I saw my old green pick-up truck and that I tried to fix it. I told her Tilly was sitting beside me now and that we were telling each other stories.

"Would you like to speak with her?" I asked Sarah, eagerly wanting to share my family with her. "She has a story to tell you."

"Alright." Sarah was being a good sport even though there really was no need for me to call her and wake her up for this conversation.

I put Tilly on the phone. "Tell Sarah your story Tilly, she'd love to hear it."

Tilly started to talk with Sarah and tell her the same story she had just told me earlier upstairs. I stayed sitting beside her with my head resting on the back of the couch as my face beamed with pride that my little niece was showing my girlfriend what a good storyteller she is.

When I got back on the phone with Sarah, she didn't sound as enthused as I had hoped. She was more concerned about what was going on with me. She still didn't think I was acting like myself. I was defensive with her and edgy when this conversation came up. At some point throughout it I let her know that I had stopped taking my Cipralex medication because I felt like I lost track of it and I didn't want to take too much. I told her I didn't know if I needed it either.

"Oh, that's what's going on," she says. "Now it all makes sense, I knew there was something." This piece of information seemed to turn into an "ah-ha" flash in Sarah's mind.

"How long have you been off of them?" she asked me.

"I'm not sure, a day or two. I stopped taking them at Diamond's cabin."

"Well, you have to start taking them again, you can't just quit them like that."

"But I don't know if I need them."

"Erin, trust me, you do, just promise me you'll start taking them again. Okay? Erin, you've been acting strange ever since you got off the plane in Calgary, something hasn't been right. You haven't been making sense."

I was offended by this. She started telling me things I was doing that were making her frustrated and I felt like I was being attacked. We got into yet another argument and my voice was raised.

The next thing I knew, Christine came pounding down the stairs in her nightgown and yelled at me like I was one of her children. "Erin, did you come here to visit or fight with your girlfriend?" She barked at me. She was very much angry with me.

Sarah had heard Christine yell at me and was saying in my ear, "we're not fighting, tell her we're not fighting."

Christine was marching around looking for her phone. She found it, dialed up the number she needed to reach and said, "Hello, this is Christine Brown calling, Gracie's mother. Gracie won't be attending school today because her aunt is visiting from Ontario. Okay, thank you. Have a nice day."

I told her I was sorry and went out the door to the shop with Sarah still on the phone. "Christine is really pissed at me."

"Well, we're not fighting."

"We kind of are," I stated, frustrated.

"Listen, I have an appointment with my nurse practitioner today, I'm going to ask her about you going off your Cipralex, and in the meantime will you promise me you'll go back on them?"

"Okay, I promise," I said.

"Okay, thank you. I will call you later today."

When I went back into the house, Christine and Tilly had both gone upstairs. I went to my blue duffel bag and searched through it to find my black bathroom supply bag where I kept my pills. I found my bottle of Cipralex, opened up the child-lock cap and took one pill out of the bottle. I swallowed it down with a glass of water and then went to lay back down on the couch. Everyone else was still upstairs in bed.

It wasn't long, maybe an hour or so, when I wanted to send Sarah a text message. I went to the plug where I thought I left my phone to charge, but it wasn't there. *Where is it? I just had it.* I started to search around the house, but couldn't see it anywhere. I went back to the plug and made sure it wasn't around there. I was getting a little frantic looking for it; frustrated, annoyed and angry with myself that it was misplaced, especially so soon after it had just been in my hands.

There was a knock on the front door. I was startled a bit and my old tendency of slight anxiety at the thought of unannounced socialism rose within me, but I pressed through it. Nobody else in the house was up so I wondered if I should just let them keep knocking. Of course, they knew we were home. I got up and opened the door to the shop, went through it, closed it and opened the door to the outside. There stood Catherine, a friend and distant neighbor, my favourite of all Christine's friends.

"So it's true, you are here," she greeted me. My anxiousness left me, but I was still riled up by not knowing where my phone was. She passed through the doorway and I greeted her with a warm hug.

"Hey, Catherine, good to see you," we smiled at each other. "Come on in, I was just searching for my phone, I just had it and now it's disappeared."

We went into the house and I kept looking for it, explaining that I was getting a little frustrated about not being able to find it. "Here," she said, offering to help, "I'll call it from my cell."

"Yeah, good idea!"

"What's the number?"

I thought for a second, but couldn't even remember my own cell phone number. I had the first three numbers, but I was stumped on the last four. I couldn't believe it. I had always known my own number, why couldn't I think of it now?

"Well, make yourself at home Catherine, do you want some coffee? Go ahead and make some, you know your way around Christine's kitchen, right?"

I kept looking for my phone. I was trying to retrace my steps, but I couldn't find it in the house anywhere. Christine got the water boiling and we made ourselves some coffee. We went out to the shop to sit down and drink it. As I went to sit down, I looked on top of Christine's car that was still sitting in the shop and there it was. My phone was sitting on top of the car's roof.

"There it is!" I exclaimed. "I must've left it out here when I got off of it with Sarah." I was elated and relieved. Catherine seemed happy for me as well.

In the meantime Christine had awoken and gotten dressed. She joined us out in the shop with her morning coffee.

I was unusually chatty, retelling Catherine the story of Allan and how I had met him in a native shelter and hung out with him for the day in Red Deer. I thought Catherine would appreciate this story seeing as in her past she and her ex had been drug addicts at one point. I showed her the pictures I had of Allan on my phone. I don't know if she noticed that I was acting more hyper than usual or not, she probably did.

At one point I turned to Christine thinking about how I will have to get back home now that I wouldn't be out here planting trees all summer. I still had some of my belongings, old books and such, stashed away in some of Christine's old vehicles that were hidden a little further up on their property. "So, what's next," I turned to Christine and asked. "Take the rest of my stuff, throw it in this car and drive back to Ontario?" It was an outlandish request, but I was serious. I could see myself doing it.

"No," Christine responded a little flabbergasted at the thought. Catherine kind of laughed to herself with the humour in the thought of me taking off cross-country with all my stuff in my sister's car. I guess it was a pretty outrageous idea, but seemed perfectly natural to me at the time. Instead, however, Catherine invited me over to her place in the next couple of days to go on the internet to book a flight back. Christine doesn't have internet access at her home.

The three of us sat and visited for most of what was left of the morning and shared our stories. I asked Catherine if she would come to my wedding that Sarah and I would be having one day. We had talked about marriage before, but not for a while.

"I'll invite you to my wedding, but only if you promise you won't hit on Sarah," I oddly stated. My filters had disappeared and I had leaked again.

"But, I'm not even gay," she explained. "I mean, I've had a couple crushes on women, but that's all." I was a little reassured by her response.

Gradually the whole house was waking up and coming alive from youngest to oldest. Lane came out and sat with us, Tilly and Kaya would come in and out at their leisure. We spent a lazy morning visiting until it came time when Catherine felt she had to go home.

Christine and I went into the house to make some breakfast, or rather brunch. The sun was beaming in her big picture window and it looked as though some of the remnants of snow would be melting away throughout the day.

My phone rings while Christine is preparing scrambled eggs. It's Sarah; she wants to talk to Christine. I hand the phone to Christine and take over the scrambled eggs. I stirred the cooking eggs, flipped the bacon around and watched to make sure the toast didn't burn in the oven. When everything was done, I plated the food for the children and brought it over to the table. We started to eat while Christine was still on the phone talking with Sarah outside of my earshot. I wasn't thinking about it. I sat down with my plate of food and began to eat. Next thing I knew Christine was sitting down to join me with her plate in her hand saying, "Well, Sarah really cares about you. You've got a good one there."

I didn't know it at the time, but Sarah had relayed to Christine the information she had gained from her nurse practitioner about what was going on with me. Sarah had told the nurse some of the things I had been doing; hanging out with some guy from the street, communicating without being logical at times or making sense, stopping to take my Cipralex, having spur of the moment ideas. The nurse practitioner had told Sarah that I'm bi-polar by the sounds of it. She had also explained to her that by going off my Cipralex cold turkey like that, if there is any underlying dormant mental illness within my brain chemistry that it could be triggered because of it. Sarah had explained all of this to my sister, not to me. Christine never told me either. I had no idea. Sarah urged Christine that I should be taken to the hospital immediately because it won't get any better, it will only get worse. Of course, Christine's vehicle was sitting in the shop and she told Sarah that it was getting fixed and she couldn't take me in right away. Again, Sarah made it clear that I needed to get to the hospital as soon as possible.

That's when Christine sat down to have brunch with me. Christine had listened to me in the past not understanding my relationships before and now she had come to the conclusion, "It's you, Erin, it's you." I wasn't sure I understood what she meant. "You're the problem in the relationship, you don't trust it and you push people away. Sarah really cares about you and you shouldn't be so worried about it, just let it be!" There's nothing like having an older sister to tell you straight up how it is.

Chapter Twelve - Drifting

Later in the day Christine and Lane had to go to town in their other vehicle to get parts for her car. Why she didn't take me to the hospital in the suburban, I don't know. My only guess is that she didn't realize the severity of what was about to unfold. Hindsight is twenty-twenty, as they say.

I was to stay and try to get some rest. She put on Edward Scissorhands for me to watch. I had never seen a movie the way I was about to see this one. Every moment of the show entranced me, like the story was being told to me in a way that meant something to my life. I was like Edward Scissorhands, a lonely naïve artist that didn't fit in anywhere. The picture and the colour seemed brighter than usual. It felt like I was on the verge of a dream where it was more vibrant and clear.

Tilly had gotten up to draw something at the kitchen table for me. When she brought it over to show me I told her how nice it was. She always signed it with her name.

At one point in the movie I got up from the couch and walked over towards the kitchen. On the old countertop someone had written "I'm crazy" in purple marker underneath a drawn picture of a clownish smiling head. I found a marker to write with, thinking this household was a free-thought dwelling that encouraged graffiti and self-expression. After the words, "I'm crazy" I wrote, "no I'm not, yes I am, no I'm not". I thought it was funny. Then I saw the square wooden mirror hanging on the wall next to the picture window. The frame was roughly 15"x20" in total with a square piece of mirror glass in the middle. This is the only mirror they had up in the house and it was a new addition since last I was here. I took it off the wall and carried it over to the couch where I had been laying before while watching the movie. It still played in the background but I was no longer paying attention to it. I had a blue bic pen in my hand and started to etch out a design on the mirror. The pen scratched away the wood, indenting it into form. I thought I would make a nice design and Christine would really like it when she got back. I scratched away; Tilly and Kaya were interested off and on in what I was doing. I was making a piece of art. With the movements of my hand, the pen scratched and flowed with ink. I got a marker and wrote in big, curly letters across the top, "What is Poop spelt backwards?" I thought it was quite witty the way I had written it. I then turned the mirror upside down and in small writing wrote, "Answer: poop." I smiled to myself and laughed inwardly. I really thought Christine was going to get a kick out of this.

I still had the mirror in my hand, filling in with the pen again and scratching out a design when Christine arrived back home. She walked up to me to see what I was doing and was shocked and angry. She grabbed the mirror from me and barked, "What are you doing? I just got that!" Christine doesn't have a lot of new nice things in her home, so she was probably glad to have a nice looking mirror hanging on her wall so she could check her hair and teeth and such, but I had ruined it. She wasn't impressed. I just shrugged my shoulders at Tilly as if I didn't know why she was so upset. Tilly shrugged them back at me. We kept watching the movie. I was thoroughly entranced by the story line again.

When Edward Scissorhands was over, Christine wanted to keep me occupied and resting, and probably out of trouble so she put something else on she thought I would enjoy. When I was a kid one of my favourite sitcoms was "Three's Company." Christine had the box set. I hadn't seen it for years. I could tell it was old just by the language they used in it; their words were pronounced just right and the structure of the sentences sounded like it was more of an old novel than what language structure we were used to on TV these days. It was different from what I remembered, but also the same. I remember watching it and thinking that some of the filming was odd. It seemed as though some of the scenes were leading into something that got cut short and not aired. I thought the show I was seeing was censored for mainstream audiences and that the seedy Hollywood people had the actors act out pornography afterwards. Perhaps they were drugged and convinced this would be a way for them to start their professional careers in acting. I never noticed this as a child, I thought. "Three's Company" was really dirty. I watched quite a few more episodes then decided I should go upstairs and try and get some actual sleep. It has been, afterall, six days now since I've actually slept.

Chapter Thirteen – Going, going…

I climbed the stairs to the unfinished upper level of the house and turned into the first bedroom just around the stairway corner to the left; Tilly and Kaya's room again. I pulled my sweatshirt over my head and placed it on the floor. Pulling back the covers I felt like this could be it, this could finally be a moment of true rest. While I laid there my thoughts took me to Allan. I started to worry about the time we spent in his van. I thought of "Big Blue", the giant oversized dildo he kept under his seat. What if he drugged me and I wasn't even aware of it. What if he drugged me and I was out while he penetrated me with "Big Blue"? Could he have had time while I was under to undress me and molest me and clothe me again before I came to? Could I have been unaware of those moments the whole time we were together? Was Sarah right? Was I in that much danger? This was all dawning on me now, the gritty and twisted reality of possibility that could have been. I put my hand under the blankets and felt for my pant line around my waist. I slipped my hand under my underwear and felt the lips of my vagina. I thought it felt strange, wider, misshapen. I took my hands out of my underwear, pulled back the blankets and stepped out of bed. Once on my feet I pulled down my pants and underwear and tried to look at my vagina. It was awkward to see. I thought I could feel a round shape in between my legs where my vagina opens. The lips of my labia looked as though "big blue" had left its indention on them, curved round around its shape. I was worried. Could it be so? I needed a second opinion.

I went downstairs in a slight inward panic. When I got down the final steps I walked over to my sister who was standing behind the couch in the living room that backed onto the open concept dining, kitchen area.

"Christine," I said in a whisper as I kept walking towards her. I didn't want anyone else to hear what I was about to ask her.

"What?" she asked.

"Christine," I continued in a whisper and got right up close to her and whispered in her ear. "Can you check my vagina to see if Allan raped me?"

"What?" she was taken aback by the request.

"I need you to look at my vagina to see if it's been raped" Christine wouldn't have known about "Big Blue", I never told her about that little bit of detail. I thought that time was of the essence if I were to know if something like that transpired. The markings would disappear in time and I needed to know if Christine saw anything.

"Erin, you weren't raped." Christine was firm and a little distressed.

"But I need you to check to make sure."

"No, don't be ridiculous. Now go back upstairs and go to bed." I did as I was told. She's probably right. The moment passed as I walked up the stairs and laid back down.

As I was laying there with my eyes closed I heard little footsteps come into the room. Lifting my head, I looked towards the end of the bed. There was little Tilly standing with a smile on her face. She jumped onto the bed and landed in a crawling position on her hands and knees. She bounced and crawled up to where I was and laid down beside me.

"Tilly, if you're going to be in here there's a no talking rule on right now, k? I really need to get some sleep, understand?"

"Yes, Erin, I'll be quiet."

"Okay, cause you'll have to go back downstairs if you're not." I closed my eyes. My whole being was tired. Some moments passed.

"Erin, your eyes are twitching." Tilly spoke in a soft voice.

I opened my eyes slowly and looked Tilly directly into hers. "Tilly, that's because I was about to dream. Eyes twitch when we go to REM sleep, rapid eye movement, and then you woke me up." I said it gently, I said it slowly hoping she would understand, but I was frustrated. I needed that sleep she had just pulled me out of.

I got out of bed and went downstairs. I walked past the little living room where Lane was sitting on one of the couches and into the open dining area. Christine was standing in the kitchen busy with some task.

"I was about to fall asleep when Tilly woke me up." I told her. She dropped whatever was in her hand on the counter a little frustrated and started to call Tilly's name.

"Tilly," she yelled up.

I didn't want Tilly to get into any trouble, she just wanted to be close to me. "Don't yell at her," I said to Christine, "she just told me my eyes were twitching and I explained to her about REM sleep." I said that part calmly and carefully. But I was losing my composure over my emotions. My eyes were tearing up and I was trying to prevent any from falling as I said, "It's been 6 days since I've slept, that's a long time to go without sleep." Lane and Christine were both looking at me when I said this but neither of them really knew what to say. I put on my boots, my jacket, my tuque, my mitts and I went outside through the kitchen door.

I was thinking that I wasn't going to be able to get the sleep I needed in the house. There were too many distractions, too many noises. I wandered over walking quickly past the garden not really sure what I was looking for or even thinking about why I had gone outside.

I went to the graveyard of old vehicles that rest off in the trees just past the garden. That's what I was looking for.

I came to an old yellow truck, four door. I put my hand on the back door handle and squeezed the square silver button in with my thumb. It was open. I pulled the door back and climbed inside, shutting it behind me. The interior smelt old and mothy. There was still garbage and remnants of things once used on the floor and on the seats. I cleared the back seat off for me to lie down on and I curled up onto it sideways trying to find a comfortable angle for my head to rest. I hugged myself with my arms for warmth. I could feel the chill of late winter, early spring around me. The air was cold yet fresh. I laid there like someone would on the street sleeping on a park bench. I was desperate. These conditions wouldn't do though. I wouldn't be able to sleep here.

I started to think about Catherine's house. I bet it would be quiet there. I sat up and thought about gathering some of my packed tree planting gear, my survivalist gear. I started making a mental note about what I would need to walk to Christine's place. I pictured walking through the woods with a compass, and knapsack filled with supplies; matches, flashlight, water, twine, hatchet, extra clothing, food. I imagined coming across a bear. I knew my thoughts were getting carried away. I knew it was a bad idea. Christine's homestead was miles and miles away.

I got out of the truck and walked with my head down back to the house, the wind blowing. Before I opened the side door I could hear Logan crying inside, scream crying. I went through the door and saw the little man with tears streaming down his cheeks, his mouth opened wide with wails coming out. Christine was still in the kitchen; Lane was out in the shop. I went straight to him and picked him up. He stopped crying almost immediately, the loud wails anyway. He nestled into my neck and sobbed with big shaken breaths as he had spent a lot of his energy. I sat down with him on the couch and rubbed his back while he settled down into low, muffled after-sobs. I kept holding him close and rubbing his back until he was asleep then I laid him down snuggly under a blanket on the couch.

I wanted to call Sarah. I unhooked my phone from the charger and dialed her up. She answered.

"Sarah?"

"Yes"

I just needed to talk to her. I told her about my thoughts of walking out across the woods to Christine's place to get some rest. I told her I knew that those thoughts were completely ridiculous, but that's what my mind was thinking. I was pacing back and forth in the dining room towards the kitchen where Christine was still preparing something. Christine was listening to my half of the conversation as I spoke to Sarah.

"Yes, I took my cipralex," I paced. I didn't realize it at the time, but I was holding on to the last strands of my conscious reality.

Chapter Fourteen – Gone

Christine put down her knife in the kitchen and said out loud, "Erin's being put into a psychosis because of a lack of sleep." This was Christine's response to hearing me talk with Sarah on the phone. Sarah was telling me about what the nurse practitioner had said of my situation.

I heard Christine say this to her family in the background, but I didn't fully take in the whole effect of what it actually meant. I was pacing back and forth while still talking to Sarah on the phone.

"I'm coming out to get you. My plane leaves tomorrow morning, early."

Something had happened in my mind that passed the point of reality at some time around now.

I still had Sarah on the line with me as I paced through the house. The children were all sitting in the living room as I paced through it. When I walked past them I told Sarah, "All the children are safe, they're sitting on the couches in the living room, all accounted for." I felt like I was patrolling the scene, taking stock of their safety, as if I was a police officer off duty. I went upstairs to talk to Sarah alone without anyone else hearing. It was then that I told her about my concerns.

"Sarah, I think the people who are renting my house are drug lords, I need you to do me a favour. Call the Beaverlodge Police Department and ask them to go over to my house and check in on it."

In my mind, asking Sarah to do this made perfect sense seeing as she worked in law enforcement. My mind had shifted to somewhere else; I was now working on the subconscious reality of things lying within it. Bits and pieces of truth in memory worked to create a story of what I thought reality was. The fact that Sarah was a jail guard and was interested in police work and the military played a role in my subconscious reality as you will see. We watched a lot of Criminal Minds together as well.

I believe the reason I brought the renters into my psychosis was because of my subconscious worry of how my house was being kept. They had moved into my house two years prior to this moment in time. I gave them the keys, they moved their stuff in and two weeks later I had moved back home to Ontario. I hadn't been in to check on them or the house since. I have wondered on occasion about how they are keeping it, but it wasn't a constant worry. When I arrived in Beaverlodge on this trip and Christine had mentioned that they had put up surveillance cameras I wasn't concerned at all at the time. It was simply information that was given to me and stored in my memory bank somewhere. I was also, obviously, not entirely myself at that time. However, perhaps this little piece of information was triggering some of my psychotic thoughts. Perhaps that is why I believed they were using my house as a drug house. My renters are a roughly mid-fifties year old woman and her thirty something year old son. I know they are heavy smokers and I know they like to drink. I also know that they are not the tidiest sort of people. Christine has passed by my house on several occasions and seen that the yard is overgrown and unkempt. My house, however, wasn't perfect either. There were some things that needed fixing, a broken window, and some unfinished work on the interior which they didn't complain about. We were even, in my mind. They paid the rent every month, sometimes in two installments, but it always showed up in my bank account. Mostly, my mind was at ease with our arrangement, until this very moment in time.

Sarah took in what I was saying and answered, "Erin, I can't do that. The cops can't just go over there and check out the house like that."

I wasn't listening to her voice of reason, I was beyond reason at this time and there was no turning back.

"Please just call them and let them know that I'm suspicious of my renters being involved in drug trafficking." I was picturing the cops there in my house at the time of saying this to Sarah. I could see it happening as I spoke of it. I wasn't calm. I wasn't rational. I was carried away. I wasn't listening to Sarah or her reasons and explanations for why calling the cops wasn't a good idea or even a possibility. Whatever she said went in one ear and out the other without a moment of processing. I was sure of what I was saying. I was sure of what I was thinking.

I walked out of Christine's bedroom while still having Sarah on the phone and went back downstairs.

"The kids are still safe in the living room." I commented to Sarah as I walked by them and carried on to the door in the shop. It was empty; I was the only one out there. I walked quickly to the other side of the car sitting there and paced back and forth while still talking to Sarah. I felt like an undercover cop planning a drug raid. I was going to be the key element in bringing it all down. There was some part of me that knew I wasn't, but I felt like I was playing in a role that I was. I was here to save the day.

My family got pulled into this psychosis. Lane was the bad guy. He was linked to the drug house operation. My mind connected him to my renters for what I believe are a couple of reasons. One, he has native heritage in him. I`m not saying that since the renters and Lane both have native blood then they are more likely to be involved in something like this. I am saying that since they shared that common ground, I linked them together as to be able to have a relationship with each other. The second reason being that Lane and I have had our ins and outs. It was easy for my mind to put him in a bad boy role. Lane, being a heavy drinker and leaving Christine at home for hours at a time played into my thinking. Their struggle for money at times and this being an easy way to make it played into my thinking. Lane is not heavy into drugs, but he does smoke pot. He`ll grow a couple plants of his own in the garden.

Basically what I'm trying to illustrate is that what you are about to read wasn't pulled from complete thin air. Instead it was taken from little bits of reality and woven together to form an unrealistic picture.

I hung up the phone with Sarah and went back into the house. I sat down at the kitchen table and thought about what to do. At this point it wasn't just a suspicion to me that my renters were doing drug deals out of my home, to me it was a definite reality. It was happening. More than that, Lane, my sister`s husband , was involved. He had kept this secret from Christine and was living a double life. I needed to save my sister and her family. I needed to take them back to Ontario with me. And I needed to do it fast. A truck, I needed a truck to throw the stuff we were taking with us into the back of it and then we could make our getaway in it. I never explained any of this to Christine, in my mind she already knew. In my mind she was planning to escape with me. I thought I saw her talking on the phone while I was sitting at the table. She seemed to be upset. I assumed she was upset because of the situation she was in, having to leave her life here finally to get away from Lane. I thought she was finally realizing that she had to leave. In reality, however, she was talking to Sarah on the phone about me and my mental state at the time.

Kaya came over to where I was sitting. I had to keep it a secret from the children. I didn't want them to be scared or upset. So I made it a game for them.

"Kaya, what do you like the most in this house? Go and bring me a couple things that you love the most and wouldn't want to be without." Since we were going to have to make such a quick getaway I wanted Kaya and the rest of the kids to be able to take a treasure with them, something that meant a lot to them as a keepsake. I asked Tilly to do the same.

The whole time I was sitting there I was thinking about my getaway plan. Lane wasn't here right now, I don't know where he was but I thought he would be on to me, finally knowing the truth about him. I knew he wouldn't just let Christine leave. I knew we had to escape in secret.

The girls brought me their favourite things from the house. They showed me pictures they had drawn.

"Good, that's good." I knew what they would want to take with them. They had their treasure, everything else could be replaced.

"Now," I said aloud to Christine, who was now off the phone, "where are the shotguns kept?" Her face filled with worry. I wanted to know where the shotguns were because I thought Lane would try to shoot me for taking his family away. It was me against him. I was willing to die trying to save my family. Christine didn't tell me, obviously, where the guns were. They were safely locked away in a cabinet somewhere.

Chapter Fifteen – The Getaway Plan

I know Christine didn't want me to upset the children. I would talk to Christine as though she knew the plan that we were escaping today. I believed Lane was fixing my old green truck at Gary's, another tidbit of reality seeping in and becoming part of my distorted truth. Lane wouldn't know that he was fixing the truck for our getaway. It had to be tonight. Sarah was going to get the cops to my house to check out the scene, and then they would know. My renters would know I was on to them and they would tell Lane. I had to get the family away before Lane was aware that I knew the truth, or else there would be trouble.

I heard the suburban coming down the laneway. Lane was home. I had to act cool. I went out to the shop and opened the outside door. Lane was looking at me as if he knew I knew. We exchanged smiles, knowing smiles. He opened the truck door and little Logan came out. I welcomed him over to me. Jacob was with his father as well. The boys were together. Lane wanted the boys and would keep them. I had Logan in my arms now. I had him. It was an offering from Lane. We could have the baby of the family. He would need his mother. Lane was going to keep Jacob. I wouldn't be able to save Jacob. Jacob would turn out like his father, a drug dealer. I brought Logan into the house. Where were the other children? I went upstairs with Logan in my arms. All the other children except for Jacob were in their parent's bedroom playing, jumping on the bed. I smiled and acted playful and cheery with them, knowing I was trying to keep a lightness in their lives that was going to be torn apart very soon. They were okay for now. I went back down stairs. Lane was sitting at the kitchen table.

I smiled when I went down and saw him there. I knew I had to pretend. I had to stay calm and play along.

Lane was trying to make conversation with me. I sat down in a chair in the living room. *Pretend. Be friendly, polite and pretend.* The TV was off. Lane was asking me about some vampire cop movie, if I had seen it or not. He wanted to put something on for me. I hadn't seen it, or heard of it. I went along with him, thinking I should feign interest in watching a movie, all the while thinking about our plan to escape.

He put on the movie for me, telling me a little about it while he did. I sat there and watched it, not remembering much or paying attention to it, just watching. Then something incredible happened. If you have ever had a lucid dream you would know how this felt, how reality shifted into a higher consciousness seemingly, how everything seemed clearer and brighter than before, that it seemed like I had awoken from sleeping while being awake. There were two cops on the screen. They were both wearing their blue uniform with a black bullet proof vest over top. Displayed on the front of their vests was a white rectangular patch. On one of the officer's patches the large block letters read "POLICE", on the other officer it read "WRITER". This was in my mind, but I was watching it on TV. It was right there in the show and it was telling me something subliminally. Sarah represented the cop, and I was the writer. The police were on their way here to get Lane. The cops had somehow linked into Christine's television set and were sending me a message. We were under surveillance. They were on their way. Sarah had been talking to them and told them what was going on, that we needed to be saved. Sarah had sent the cops here. It was clear; everything in my mind was crystal clear. The undercover operation was going as planned. They had been to my house and seen that they were involved in selling drugs. They shut them down and now they were on their way for Lane. And I was supposed to be a writer and Sarah was supposed to be a cop. She has a cop personality. That's why the vests read what they did. We were working together as a team. I am in control. I am in charge. I am a force to be reckoned with.

I'm ready to confront Lane. He's having a beer at the kitchen table. *He's distressed. He knows his time is up.* He looks at me and takes a big sip from his bottle.

"Erin, why don't you have a beer?" *No, I will not have a beer. He wants me to have a beer so he can drug me, keep me contained, and control me through alcohol and whatever else he puts in it.*

"Nobody is drinking anything. NO DRINKS!" I was firm and aggressively calm. Lane was no match for me, I would handle this. He took another swig from his bottle and seemed physically fidgety, nervous. I was challenging him and his authority in this house. He would no longer be in control. He would no longer keep this family possessed by him and in the dark about who he really is.

"Okay, just try to stay calm, Erin, you should maybe just have a beer and relax a bit." *A beer and relax? Who did he think I was, some ignorant bumpkin easily swayed into believing whatever he would tell me?*

"NO, NOONE IS HAVING ANY DRINKS, YOU GOT THAT? NO DRINKING!" I was in his face and he didn't like it. He got up from his chair. This was it. This was the moment I had to handle. He knows I know now. I won't take the drink, so he knows I know. He's getting up to challenge me.

I put my hands on his shirt and pulled him back towards the staircase. I push him up against the descending frame and yell in his face, "I WILL DIE FOR THIS FAMILY!" I put my hands around his neck. He puts his around mine. "YOU WANT TO CHOKE ME, HUH? YOU WANT ME TO PASS OUT SO YOU CAN STICK YOUR DICK IN MY MOUTH? I'M NOT GOING TO SUCK YOUR DICK!" I have no idea why I was yelling like this to Lane. Why was I being so vulgar and obscene? I kept yelling and talking in this manner while I held him in a strangle position. Lane was scared. He didn't want to fight back, but he couldn't let me strangle him.

I felt super human in my strength. The fact that Lane was a 6 foot tall man who worked physically hard all of his life didn't phase me. I felt like I could overcome him physically. My mental state made me incredibly strong. Lane freed himself from me somehow.

I have no recollection of doing what I am about to tell you. Christine informed me after the fact that I started to skip around the house singing a very sexually obscene song. I sang it all over the house for I don't know how long. Hopping and skipping and singing explicit things as if it was a childish song even though the content was extremely adult. I went upstairs singing and came back down again.

My memories lose a lucid flow to them now. I remember chopped bits and specific moments in time.

Christine and I go out the side door and head towards the outhouse. It's dark now. It feels as though we're frantic and aware that we might be in danger. I think of Christine being trapped here so long unaware of her situation and being controlled into thinking this is all she can have. Lane pushed her into a mental state of defeat. She didn't have the strength to leave on her own. She needed me to help her. I believed Lane controlled her by yelling at her loudly like a bear breathing down on her with its arms outstretched intimidating her into feeling like nothing. These were my thoughts as we walked through the wooded path to the outhouse where Christine took a pee. This, obviously, is not the truth.

Lights are seen coming up the driveway. A vehicle was on its way in. Who was it? Christine wiped herself and pulled up her pants. We went to investigate who was here. Lane was outside talking to whoever was in the big white truck.

"It's Troy and Anne," Christine said as we got close. She recognized the vehicle. They just happened to drop by for a neighborly visit, but I thought they were here to help. I thought Christine called them over to help us get away from Lane. We had to still be secretive about it. Lane wouldn't know they were here to help us.

I greeted them. It had been a couple of years since I had last seen them. We all went into the house.

Troy and Anne sat down at the kitchen table. Christine offered tea. "No, nobody is having anything to drink," I wouldn't allow it. It wouldn't have taken Troy and Anne long to figure out something was wrong.

Lane had returned to his spot at the head of the table and continued to take big gulps of his beer. "You want a beer? Tea? Water?" Lane was trying to find a way for us to all relax. "Let's just sit down and have some tea."

I was standing behind him and put my hand on his left shoulder. "No one is having anything to drink." Lane tried to stand up, but I pushed him back down into his chair.

"Jesus Christ," he said as he took another big swig from his bottle of beer.

"I've got some friendship cake here," Christine said, "let's have some of that."

"No, no one is having any cake." I thought I was protecting everyone from being drugged. We finally had Lane right where we wanted him. He was finally going to be caught and I wasn't going to make a mistake now.

I had Sarah on the phone now. She told me an ambulance is on the way. Good, I thought, in case Lane tries to kill me. I kept her on the phone. The phone was tapped and she had the cops listening in on our conversation. They were there to make sure that if Lane or I were killed, they would know what happened.

I told Sarah that nobody is drinking. I wanted the cops to hear that so they didn't think any of the information was getting mixed up. I relayed information to her, "Troy and Anne are here, they're sitting at the kitchen table with Lane. Lane is here in the house and Christine and Jacob are here too. I don't know where the girls are. I think they must be upstairs."

"It's okay," I say to Troy and Anne, "Sarah is a jail guard." Troy and Anne look at me and nod their heads.

The cake is on the table. "Did anyone eat the cake?" I ask in a frenzy, Sarah is still on the line in my ear.

"Erin, the cops are on their way too. It's going to be okay."

"Jacob," I look at Jacob who is standing in the kitchen. "Did you eat any of the cake, Jacob?" I started to walk closer to him.

"No," he says, straight-faced.

I'm right up to him now and looking him right in the eyes. "Did you eat the cake?"

"No"

"Did you eat the cake?" I'm beginning to raise my voice.

"No", Jacob kept answering my badgering question calmly while looking directly into my eyes.

I'm screaming it at him now, "DID YOU EAT THE CAKE? DID YOU EAT THE CAKE?" I was acting as though I was Lane screaming in their faces. It was a test I was conducting to see if he would crack under the pressure of having me yell it in his face.

"No," Jacob replied again, just as calmly as he did the first few times. I was satisfied. Sarah was still on the phone but I wasn't talking to her anymore, she was just there for the phone tap. She had to stay on the line so the cops knew what was happening here. It had to be on record. Lane was going to jail.

I told Troy and Anne how they were good people. They were good neighbors. I was in control of this situation.

Red and blue lights were in the driveway.

"They're here," I told Sarah. "The cops are here." I could let her go now; they were here, so I could let her go.

Chapter Sixteen – Lock Down

I went and sat down in the living room. Troy came over to talk to me. He was talking gently and soothingly as if to calm me down. I wanted Anne to be with him, I didn't want to talk to Troy alone, Anne had to be next to him. She came and sat on his knee. I felt better.

I had tiled Troy and Anne's bathroom before I left for Ontario two years ago. Christine had told me once that the grout was falling out of the joints. I asked Troy about that now. He said "No, it isn't" and seemed to wonder why I would even think about such a thing happening.

Christine told me afterwards that when the cops had arrived her and Lane went outside to greet them. She told me that I came outside and when one of the cops came up to them and asked what the problem was I said, "I'll tell you what the problem is, her husband is an asshole." Then apparently I said, "I'm a trickster," and started to skip up the laneway while singing a song.

I remember skipping up the laneway and I remember singing a song. I was making up the lyrics and melody at that moment. I was singing it with all my heart. I stopped skipping and began to walk, still singing my song. I felt like I was really expressing myself. I thought about all the times I was alone with my music, just me and my guitar and some melody or lyric that I was creating. I felt like those moments are what gave me the strength to keep going when times or emotions got hard. It was my creative expression that gave any kind of meaning or grace to my life. That is why I am singing now. I needed strength. I kept walking up the laneway towards the road and I felt alone.

It was quiet when I stopped singing. So quiet I could hear my footsteps crunching as I walked forward. When I came around the little bend near the end of the laneway I saw flashing lights at the end of it. I wasn't quite sure what it was at first. I stopped and looked up ahead. There were two people in uniform standing beside a parked ambulance on the road right in front of my sister's laneway. Once I realized this I turned around and began walking back towards the house.

When I got back up close to the house a police officer came over to me and took my arm. He walked me over to the right side of the four-door police pick-up truck and his partner opened the back door. Lane was inside. He was over on the left side of the truck with his hands behind his back and a little grin on his face. He inched over and the cop that opened the door helped him to get out. They unlocked the handcuffs that were around his wrists. Lane looked at me, still smiling, and put his arms out to the sides while he made a big shrug of the shoulders. The cops then turned me around, pulled my arms back and attached the handcuffs onto my wrists. They put me in the backseat of the police truck.

This was a game to me; a game to figure out how to get out of the handcuffs and out of the police cruiser. Lane had done it. He showed me that it was possible to escape. I wasn't in trouble, I was in some kind of riddle where I had to use my wits to figure it out.

Below the glass and grate barrier between the front seat and me there was a silver plated backing on the backs of the chairs. I started to tap my feet on it as if I was doing a dance. As I got more and more into the flow of the movements of my feet, I tapped danced all the way up the plated backing turned myself over onto my backside and continued to tap dance on the roof of the truck. Feverishly and passionately I was clicking and clacking my boots on the metal roof. I would figure out this game. I would get out. I started to hoof at the right side door that I was let in on. With big double footed kicks I was going to knock the door open. I did that a few times then started to tap dance on the ceiling again. Turning around I started to hoof at the other backseat door. My work boots landed with a powerful crunch against the silver plated metal interior. I wasn't stopping this time until the door was opened. With a sudden movement the door was open and a large male police officer was standing there. He had opened it. I stood up on the ground out of the truck with my hands still cuffed behind my back. With a powerful force he thrust his hand towards my chest and pushed me backwards into the truck, slamming the door behind me.

I sat back up on the seat and looked out the window. Christine was talking to the police officers. She looked upset. I looked towards the house. In the big picture window I saw Anne looking out and then I saw Troy walk over and look out beside her. Anne put her head down and walked away from the window.

My mood was happy and excited. My mind had created yet another unrealistic tale to tell me. These police officers were friends of Sarah's. She knew them way back in college when she was taking police foundations. They were here to pick me up and take me to my little house in Beaverlodge where we were going to get married. All of my family and friends were going to be there, from the east and the west, as well as all of Sarah's family and friends. In fact, they were already there waiting for me to arrive. I was to arrive in this police truck cruiser with my hands handcuffed behind my back and Sarah had the key to unlock me. If I was really good, I could somehow figure out how to get the cuffs off before I got there. If I did that she would be really impressed. I would be like Houdini.

In reality, Sarah had told me on the phone that she was going to come out to get me. She knew I was headed to the hospital and she had been making plans to come out and stay at a hotel in order to be there to take me back home. She told me that her and her mom had rearranged our little apartment so that our stuff could fit in there better and we would have more room to breathe. I would have more room to practice my guitar. We would be more comfortable.

I had taken that bit of information and turned it into Sarah and her mom had rearranged my house in Beaverlodge to prepare for the wedding. I had no thoughts as to where the renters were; somehow they just let them take over the house so we could get married in it.

When the cops got back in the truck, turned it around and started to drive up the laneway I was elated and excited. I couldn't believe I was going to get married. Christine and Lane and the kids and Troy and Anne and all the others were going to meet us there. Everyone I had ever known while living out west was going to be there. My mom and all my family from back east were all going to be there too at my house. They were all waiting for me to arrive. What a celebration we were about to have. When the two cops got in the truck and started to turn around to go back out the laneway, I was glad to be hitting the road.

I thought of trying to bring my arms down around my butt so my hands were in front of me. If I did that then I could work on the cuffs. It felt like too much effort though. I wanted to relax. I was going to hide from Sarah so she didn't see me right away. Then, I would jump out and surprise her. I lay down on the back seat of the truck. Face down. I was hiding. I got tired of lying like that so I turned around and lay on my back with my arms behind me. I was laying there thinking of getting married. Wait a minute. I have my period. I wonder if I have a period stain between my legs. I don't want that. I tapped on the glass barrier with my foot. The cop in the passenger seat slightly turns his head. I tapped again. This time he turns around and opens the sliding glass window while looking at me lying there.

Trying to be discreet, I ask in a quiet voice, "Do I have any blood in my crotch." He looks at my face. I open my legs for him to see. He looks.

"No" he says without expression, looks at my face again then shuts the window and turns around.

Good, I thought. I can't have that on my wedding day. Sarah MacLoghlin, I'm marrying Sarah MacLoghlin. Holy shit, I can't believe it. She's Sarah McLachlan! I'm marrying Sarah McLachlan, the folk singer. She completely went undercover to start a new life away from the media and the spotlight and has become a new person with a new identity. She shaved her head, and started a whole new career and now I'm marrying her. I've found my musical soulmate. We're going to make the sweetest music together.

I was watching the familiar countryside pass me by and thought of how lucky I am to be marrying my soulmate. I wanted a cigarette. I would like to stop and take a moment before my wedding. I don't know if I'm ready just yet. This was going to be the biggest union of my life. I was feeling a little cold-footed the closer we got. I wonder if these guys, these police officers would mind if we had a smoke before we got to the house. I wonder if they have any cigarettes, seeing as I don't. Beaverlodge is just up ahead, I'm not ready.

When we passed Beaverlodge on the highway I was confused at first. I didn't know why we weren't going to my house. We must be early. We have to put in some time before showing up. Maybe I'll have a cigarette after all.

We were headed towards Grande Prairie. As the time passed I wove together another story to explain what we were doing and where we were headed. They're taking me to the Crystal Centre in Grande Prairie where Sarah and I are going to put on a huge concert together. She's going to play all her old songs and I'm going to play mine. I'm going to go up on stage and join her. This is pretty exciting. Everyone is going to be there. I still can't believe that my Sarah MacLoghlin is THE Sarah McLachlan! Incredible!

Before we head over to the concert, though, we're going to stop in at Fen's place. I'm going to invite her to the concert. She was the first person I truly loved and I want her to be there and partake in this glorious celebration. I'll go to her house and we'll have a cup of tea and talk about the love we shared in the past. This will be my way of saying goodbye to her, the girl I wanted to marry so many years ago. I was happy that she was going to be there: My one true love.

I wasn't able to keep track of where we were once we were in the city of Grande Prairie. Part of me still thought we were circling around putting in time before going to the wedding. The other part of me thought we were headed to the big concert.

The truck pulled up to a stop in front of the Emergency Doors. It was bright here. The lights of the hospital made the darkness of the night bright. I registered that we were at a hospital, but not why.

I leaned forward in the truck; the glass window was slid open. "I know you from somewhere," I said to the young skinny boy cop with the shaved head sitting in the passenger's seat.

He looked at me with a straight face and said, "The mosh pit".

I thought about Lollapalooza the year I saw Hole headlining and thought, "Yeah, that could be it."

My right side door was opened and I was to get out. The change in my pocket, my wallet and my phone had fallen onto the leather seats.

"Should I get my things?" I asked the police officers.

"Just leave it, we'll gather it up." They each took one of my arms and walked me towards the sliding doors. I was being escorted into the backstage part of the concert I was about to be in. Sarah was already onstage.

Walking through those doors with a police officer on each arm I must have looked like Jack Nicholson when he was delivered into the psych ward in "One Flew Over The Cuckoo's Nest". I had a huge grin on my face and smiled at the nurse's attending behind their desk. All eyes were on me when I came through and was escorted past the front desk. They put me into a brightly lit room close to the nursing station. Somebody asked me to empty my pockets and take off my boots. They shut the door behind me.

Chapter Seventeen – The Bright Room

I needed a shower; I had to clean myself up before the show. I started to take my clothes off; piece by piece my garments fell to the floor. There was a door beside the sink where I thought the shower would be. I tried to open it, but it was locked. I looked out the long skinny window of the door that I was brought in through and about 40 meters away I saw the nursing station. I could see the two cops that brought me in talking to women in scrubs. One of the cops looked over towards me. I needed to get dressed again. I can't shower. I put on my bra and my shirt. I reached down for my underwear and slipped them over my feet one at a time. I needed to go pee. I looked under the sink that was attached to the wall between both doors and saw a drain. I lifted the cover of the big industrial drain and crouched under the sink. I was careful to direct my urine directly into the oversized round hole. I shook myself off as best I could before standing out from the drain and pulling my underwear up to my hips. I pulled on my pants and zipped them up. Then I bent back down to handle my dirty stinking socks and pulled them back onto my feet.

I was starting to question what this place was. I thought I was supposed to be held here so I could get freshened up before the show, but there was no shower. So, what was I doing here? I looked around the room. It was about 100 sq ft. It had a hospital bed pushed up against the back wall, some kind of silver metal cabinet hanging on the left wall, nothing on the right and a sink in between the two doors. That was it. It was a white room; a very brightly lit white room.

There was nothing for me to do so I decided to lie down on the firm hospital bed and close my eyes.

I don't know if I slept or not. I don't know what time I was brought in there either, I just know it was night time. Time was elusive in this room. It was always the same time, bright time.

I opened my eyes and stayed lying down with my hands behind my head. I was resting under a thin hospital sheet. Thoughts of a concert were no longer there, they had vanished. It felt as though I was being tested somehow. My mind drifted to another resolution explaining the situation I was in. I was in a military training camp. My superior intelligence and physical prowess was perfectly suited for military duties. I was being trained for the psychological endurance needed to survive being held hostage in an enemy's camp. I would need to be able to think under pressure in life threatening situations and somehow free myself from seemingly impossible circumstances. Right now I am in training. This was a waiting room, a holding room, but everything is a test.

My years spent as a treeplanter, living in the woods away from society, was good training. I learned survivalist skills. I was able to toughen the elements out. I honed in on my ability to create solutions to existing problems using the available resources, which might not be much. All of this brought me here.

I needed a shower. I wanted to be clean. I wanted to be fresh. I got up out of the bed and walked over to the door with the window to outside of this room. It was quiet out there. There weren't as many lights on as there was before. Sitting in a chair just before my door there was an older lady with dark hair. She was dressed in scrubs and brown in skin. She was native. While she was looking at me looking at her, I motioned for her to open the door. She shook her head no. She was kind, gentle, I could tell. I motioned for her to come here and open the door. I was very calm and mild mannered. She hesitated and opened the door a tiny crack so that my head could speak to her head.

"Can I have a shower?"

She spoke with a soft voice, a motherly voice, "No. You can have a shower when you go upstairs."

"Oh, okay." I didn't really register what she meant. I just knew I wasn't allowed to have a shower.

"Are you here to look after me?"

"Yes," she said a little timidly.

"Oh, so you're like my mama bear for the night," I beamed a smile at her.

She smiled back and laughed slightly, "Yes, I suppose so."

"Well, that's what I'll call you then, Mama Bear." I was happy to meet her. She smiled again and then brought the door back to a close at the end of our conversation. I liked Mama Bear. I would see her face looking in through the glass on me often.

At some point someone who I'm assuming was a nurse came in. She introduced herself to me. I told her about having to pee in the drain. I apologized. She looked at the drain and then at the door beside the sink.

"Oh, I'm sorry," she says as she takes her card and swipes it in front of the black box hanging on the wall beside the door. The little light turns from red to green. She turns the knob of the door and opens it. It's a toilet stall. "This should have been opened earlier for you." She had to prop the door open with something or else it would just lock itself shut again. She took a towel that was resting on my bed and placed it on the floor between the door jam and the door. It stayed open a crack.

"Thank you," I said. She left as soon and abruptly as she had come.

A little while later the door opened and a young nurse came in with a telephone in her hand. "Do you know who Sarah MacLoughlin is?" She asked me.

"Yes, she is my girlfriend."

"You have a phone call," she said, looking at me with a sparkling glint in her eye. "It's Sarah," she told me and passed me the hand held phone before leaving the room and closing the door. Apparently, it was around midnight.

"Hello," I said into the receiver.

I heard the concern and worry in Sarah's voice as she greeted me, "Erin? Are you okay? I've been trying to get in touch with you but they wouldn't let me talk to you."

"Yes, I'm okay, I'm good, how are you?" This was just like any other conversation I was having. There was no need for the urgency in her voice; I was fine, no big deal.

"Where are you, what's been going on?"

"I'm in this little room." My voice was chipper, just pure happiness. "There's a lady who is taking care of me. She's like my mom making sure I'm okay. I call her Mama Bear. Everyone is really nice; they're all looking after me. I had to go to the bathroom earlier when I got here and I didn't have a toilet handy, so I had to pee under the sink in the drain, but I told the nurse about it." I could hear how upset Sarah was, she had even begun to cry. "Sarah, why are you crying?"

"I didn't know what was happening with you. I was worried about you. I had to fight with the nurses just to let me talk to you. I told them you're my spouse and that we live together and I AM immediate family, but they wouldn't listen to me. Finally I said, 'Listen, we're gay. I don't know about you and what goes on out there in Alberta, but here in Ontario where I'm from I get equal rights and I want to talk to my girlfriend.' She finally said 'okay, fine, hold on."

"Sarah, I know there's something wrong with me."

"Yes, Erin, there is, but it's going to be okay. You're there to get some help."

"Yeah, yeah they're going to help me, I know, but don't cry, everything is fine." Nothing about the situation seemed to bother me.

"Well, you're going to be talking to a psychiatrist. Just tell her everything that's happened."

"Okay," was my nonchalant response. I was listening to her but I still didn't really know what was going on. I was in my own little world where everything was happy and okay. I'm sure I was glad that she was coming, but I wasn't aware of the significance as to why.

We didn't talk long. When we had said our goodbyes I hung up the phone and looked out the window of my door to let Mama Bear know I was done. She opened the door and took the phone away from me.

I lay back down on the bed for a time, again not knowing if I slept.

~

Clean. I wanted to be clean. I decided to wash my hair in the sink. I turned on the taps to a temperature I liked and plunged my head under it. It felt good. I had two towels on the bed. I knocked on the door gently to talk to Mama Bear. She opened it slightly for me again.

"Can I have some soap?"

"What do you want it for?"

"I want to wash my hair."

"Ok," she closed the door.

A few moments later she opened it again and gave me a little cup half filled with yellow goo; my soap. I thanked her before she closed the door tight again.

It felt good to lather my hair with the soap she had given me. I washed it out in the sink and patted the sopping drips out with my white towel afterwards. That was better; now for my clothes. My shirt stank like sweat I thought. I took my t-shirt off and wore only my white ribbed old man tee that was underneath. Still feeling like I was in military training, I imagined this is how I would have to bathe out in the field. There wouldn't be any cushy showers out there in the trenches of military work. I would have to make due with what I have and right now I have a toilet. I plunged my shirt in the toilet bowl to wash it. I don't know why I didn't wash it in the sink like I did my hair, I didn't think of it, I only thought of the toilet water.

Mama bear opened the door and looked around the corner at me. "What are you doing?" she asked.

"Washing my clothes," I smiled back, proud of myself. She looked at me and decided I wasn't doing any harm and backed back out of the room.

I continued washing my shirt and rang out the water. I hung it up on the open bathroom door, making sure the towel was still lying bunched up on the floor so the door wouldn't lock on me.

I motioned to talk to Mama Bear again, and she opened the door slowly to listen to me. "Can I have a toothbrush and some toothpaste?"

She nodded her head and slowly closed the door again. I think she was beginning to see that I was harmless. When she brought me the supplies I had asked for I proceeded to brush my teeth. I finally felt refreshed and like I was passing some kind of test; a test of my endurance and strength and resourcefulness. I would be able to face a prisoner of war camp. I would be able to endure the torture they could potentially bestow upon me.

A chipper nurse opened the door and greeted me with a roll in dinner table. I was confident around the young girl and politely thanked her. She smiled a friendly smile, told me to enjoy it and left. There were magazines on the table as well. I placed them on the bed, sat down beside them, pulling the dinner cart over towards me.

My movements were slow and methodical. I was inspecting the tray. I saw a glass of orange juice and a brown plastic cup with a plastic lid to match on it. Beside the cup was a red rose tea bag, a packet of sugar and a plastic cup with a little bit of milk filling the bottom. I had two pieces of toast that I could see and jam packets. I lifted the plastic lid sitting on my plate of food slowly and looked under it to find scrambled eggs and sausages. This would do just fine. I ate everything, drank everything and enjoyed it all.

After the nurses took the tray away I laid back down on top of the bed and began sifting through the magazines they had left for me. They weren't my kind of reading. One was some kind of girly fashion magazine which I completely ignored. The other had more of a political slant to it so I decided to peruse through its pages. It wasn't the articles that caught my attention though, it was the advertisements. Everything in that magazine, especially the advertisements, felt surreal to me. I literally felt like this is how your perceptions would feel if you had died and gone to heaven. They seemed more intelligent, clearer and as though the messages they were giving were more meaningful.

I'm sure we've all heard theories of what it is like when we die. One of those theories is that "heaven" is very similar to earth except everything is much more beautiful and utopic; the architecture, the landscape. I imagine the complete bliss that one's spirit could hold would be incredible in a heavenly state. While sifting through this magazine I caught a glimpse of that feeling of being highly evolved and in a perfect state of being. These glimpses felt like a utopian society can truly exist if we are aligned with our spirit and true desires. At this point in time my true desire was to be trained in the military; to be physically challenged and mentally challenged in heroic ways. The advertisements seemed like they were of a different advertising breed; they were more sophisticated.

Still, I grew tired of the magazine. I just laid there on the cot and looked around the room. On the bottom of the metal cabinet, hanging on the wall by my head, I could see a hole with a strange shaped metal object dangling out from it. I looked at it some more. I got up out of the bed to inspect it more closely.

It was an oddly shaped hunk of metal freely hanging from the cut out hole on the bottom of the cabinet. I thought that if I could somehow keep moving the object around I would eventually be able to find a way to pull the object out of the hole and it would be free; like a shape test. If I could do this then I thought I would be able to open the cabinet and see what was inside. Again, I thought this was some kind of test of my intelligence. I played around with my puzzle for a few minutes thinking I would pass the test and I was happy to have the challenge. I rotated and turned the metal object around, seeing its shape on its hidden end more through the hole that contained it. I was completely occupied by it. It wasn't long, however, before Mama Bear opened the door and asked me what I was doing. I smiled at her and let her know that I was trying to get the object out of the hole. I was proud of myself. She told me in a gentle way not to do that. I was a little disappointed, I thought I was doing good, but I accepted her authoritative position over me and abided by her request. I guess it wasn't a test. I was a little confused.

I lay down and waited, for what, I don't know.

Chapter Eighteen – What's Up, Doc?

There was a group of nurses outside my door. I could see them through the glass window. They were talking with a man. This man seemed in a hurry. The nurses seemed like they were trying to stop him, but he persisted. My door opened. He came in.

He had brought a chair with him and placed it down on the floor a little in front of my bed, where I was sitting up and looking at him.

He introduced himself to me as being a psychiatrist. He was a doctor, and he wanted to speak with me and ask me a few questions. I was okay with this.

He had told me his name, but I kept thinking he must be Dr. Lit, the psychiatrist my brother had when he was staying in the Homewood in Guelph. But he told me another name. Perhaps they are related.

I asked him if he was Dr. Lit, but he said no. I asked him if they were related or if he knew him. Again, he said no with a curious look on his face. I told him who Dr. Lit was, my brother's old psychiatrist. They were both Asian, that's why I thought they could be the same person. And my mind, at this time, believed that people's identity can change slightly, perhaps be reborn into a new life while still having a part of their old one, not necessarily through death, but through a conscious re-birth.

When he was finished interviewing me, he politely, yet reservedly said goodbye and left the room. He took the chair with him.

~

A little while later I had another visitor. She came through the door with professional confidence and ease. She, too, was carrying a chair and placed it in front of me before the bed. She was wearing a long white coat over her clothing. She sat down, told me her name, said that she, too, was a psychiatrist and then simply asked me to tell her how I came to be here.

"Well, how far back do you want me to go?" I asked her.

"As far back as you want," she replied.

I remember telling her about the breakdown of Diamond's truck. I told her about some things that happened while I was waiting in Red Deer. Other than that, I'm not sure what I told her.

She simply listened to me speak and relay the events of my story. She asked me a few other questions and I answered as best I could. I knew she was a psychiatrist, I comprehended that. I felt like I was doing a good job at describing how I got to this place. I didn't know she was attempting to diagnose me at this time. I was being studied by her as I spoke.

It didn't take her long.

Chapter Nineteen - Upstairs

Mama Bear opened my door. "They're ready for you upstairs," she told me, "they have a room for you."

I was given back my possessions. In a plastic tray there was the little toy truck Logan had given me, a bottle cap with a beaver on it and some loose change. I put it all in my pockets. My wallet and cell phone would be locked away for me for the time being. My boots were handed to me; I put them on.

I pulled my damp t-shirt down from the bathroom door. I was wearing my sweatshirt over top of my old man tee.

I was ready to move. Mama Bear was my guide. I followed her through the emergency hospital wing.

There was a man sitting on the end of a hospital bed in one of the sections. He looked like a hard-working man. I looked at his finger; it had a cast over it with an excessive amount of bandages over his hand and a sling on his arm. I thought to myself, 'that's a bit overdone for just a broken finger.' I looked at him with a smirking smile. He looked back at me and shook his head slowly back and forth. We were thinking the same thing.

Mama Bear and I got on the elevator. We went up to the fifth floor.

When the doors of the elevator opened there was a nursing station desk just over to the left. We took a few steps over to it and Mama Bear let them know who I was. I was greeted with kindness.

This was as far as Mama Bear could go. I had to pass through the secure doors without her. So, I thanked her for all she had done for me and said goodbye to my Mama Bear. I then went through the doors.

On the other side there was a large room with natural light coming through from the other side. The whole back wall was glass windows. There was a sitting area with a television set directly in front of me.

Beyond that there was a Ping-Pong table and a games area where there were shelves of board games. The nursing station was on the left side of the entrance door and in the middle of the room; double doors were on either side of the station leading to the eating area and the patient rooms.

The nurse showed me which room was mine. I had a single. All I could think about was that now I could finally get clean. "Can I have a shower?" I asked the nurse.

I didn't have a change of clothes, so the nurse guided me back through the double doors past the nursing station and across the open games and lounge area. Beyond this large room was a hallway with several other rooms. One of which was a music room. The nurse was unlocking a door on the other side of the hall with one of her keys.

"Go ahead and pick an outfit out," she said softly. "There's lots to choose from."

Shelves of clothing were before me; jeans, t-shirts, sweaters all neatly stacked and organized into piles. It didn't take me long to pick out a pair of jeans and a red plaid short sleeved snap button shirt. I also took an extra old fashioned knitted sweater that would have been popular in the seventies. I was grateful for the new clothes.

I asked the nurse where my cell phone and wallet were. She took me back out of the room, locking the door behind her, and showed me around the corner towards the large lounge area. There she let me know that my belongings were safely locked away in this large cabinet and that I will be given them back when I'm ready to leave. She opened one of the doors with her key and showed me my wallet and cell phone. I looked at her and nodded my head in approval. I knew they were safe.

While the nurse was showing me where my belongings were, an agitated and angry man walked over to the cabinet with another nurse. He was shaking his head in disapproval of something. He wanted something that he could not have and he was not impressed by it.

The nurse then led me back to her station and gave me a toothbrush, some toothpaste, some soap, shampoo and a towel. She informed me as to where the showers were, just off the dining area, and off I went.

I walked back through the double doors on the right side of the nursing station. Just past them on the other side, I could see an empty room with a mattress on the floor and dishevelled blankets. This wasn't an ordinary room; it had glass walls to look in on and nothing but the mattress inside it. It gave me a slightly eerie feeling.

I kept walking forward. Resident's rooms were all lined up on the periphery of the dining area. It's a small ward, with a little more than a handful of patients. I walked past the two-man tables on the left and found the washroom and shower area. Just beyond where I turn to go into the shower there is a nursing attendant sitting outside of someone's room watching over them. I smile at her and say hello as I open the door and disappear into the ladies shower room.

Through those doors I walk in onto the tiled floor. There are a few bathroom stalls, and across from them a counter with a couple sinks in front of a large mirror. A woman is standing in front of one of the sinks and putting make-up on in the mirror. She doesn't acknowledge my presence. Just to the left a little beyond the entrance there is a curtain pulled back revealing a shower stall.

I step over the tiled step into the little change area of the shower and put my clothes and supplies down on the wooden bench. I close the curtain behind me and begin to take my clothes off and place them next to my new, clean clothes. Reaching in past the curtain of the shower I turn on the water and let the temperature reach its warmth. I step in. I was a little rushed and excitable in my shower.

My thoughts were not calm, but I was in the moment. I don't know if I really even thought about where I was or why I was here, I just was.

When I was finished cleaning myself I towelled myself off and got dressed. I went over to the sink to brush my teeth and fix my hair. Then I gathered up my old clothes and things and walked out towards my room to drop them off.

I made my room home. I put my clothes in the dresser and took out my little toy truck that Logan gave me and put it on the nightstand next to the beaver head bottle cap. The cap reminded me of Christine's place.

Once I felt like I had made myself at home in my little private hospital room I was ready to leave it. I felt proud of myself for being so organized, not really a trait I'm known for.

I walked out to the common area, taking the scenery in. I remembered there was a music room, so I went to investigate that more. It was empty, no one was in there and it felt like nobody had been in there for a long time. There was a piano and a guitar leaning on its stand next to some chairs. I walked over and sat down next to the guitar, picking it up as soon as I had sat. It was an acoustic, which I was accustomed to playing. I held it in my hands and plucked each string individually to hear if it was in tune. Not bad, I thought to myself. It only needed a few minor adjustments.

Whenever I have a guitar in my hand the songs that come to mind to play are the ones I have written. I never usually have an audience, so I feel comfortable playing them. I was alone in this room and so I played one of my own songs.

I played the song I tribute to my grandmother, "Just One Look". It's a country song about a little girl who admires the marriage of her grandparents and wants to know who she will marry someday. It tells the background of how her grandparents met and how they lived their life on a farm.

I played two songs while I was there and that was enough for me. I didn't have the will or desire to play anymore. I put the guitar back down on its stand and left the room. Before I got far, I heard the voice of a lady complimenting my playing. I turned around to see a nurse smiling at me. She sounded very sincere and I was humbled and grateful for the compliment. I never know how the music and singing sounds to other people's ears.

I walked around the corner to look out the large windowed wall. I could see a lot of the city from here. I stood in front of the benches and chairs that were lined up in front of it and looked out for a little while at the buildings and the skyline; the big and vast beautiful skyline. I turned my head to see the bookcase of games and magazines. I perused through its shelves and saw a deck of cards sitting on top of it next to a cribbage set. I immediately thought of Gracie and the card trick she showed me. I took the deck of cards and thought that I would make up a trick so the next time I saw her I would have it ready to show her.

I sat down cross-legged on the bench in front of the large windows with my back turned towards the nursing station. I started to take the cards out of the deck and collect only the ones I wanted. Gracie's deck only had three's in it; I was trying to copy something similar to that. I sifted out and kept all four Kings, all four Queens, all four Aces, and all four Jacks. I also kept the two Jokers. I put the rest of the cards in a pile out of the way. In front of me on the bench I turned my selection face up so I could see them all. I was contemplating how I could somehow predict the card someone would pick knowing it was only these cards. I knew I needed more of the same, but I only had these ones for now. I was completely enthralled with trying to figure some kind of trick out when a nurse came over to me and told me it was lunch time.

"Can I leave my cards here?"

"Sure you can."

I chose to take them with me though. I put the other cards back on the shelf and put the cards I wanted to use in my pocket.

When I walked through the double doors on the right side this time I could see a woman in scrubs sitting at a little table with a book in her hands. She was sitting outside the glass room. I looked in the windows and saw the angry man sitting down on the mattress. He looked at me with a scowl still on his face and shook his head. He was really not impressed with something. I stood there looking at him wondering why he was so upset. I chatted with the lady sitting on watch over him while I looked in on this man. I thought about wanting to go in there, if only I could talk with him and find out what was wrong. Maybe I could help him. I don't know how she could tell, but a nurse behind me a little further up the hall from where I had just walked called out to me, "Erin, don't go in there." I looked at her, then I looked in at him and I decided to keep walking.

When I got to the little eating area there were already a handful of people sitting and eating with their tray of food. I looked to see a tall silver cart with little shelves over on the other side. I walked over and looked at the trays of food; they were all organized by the patient's name. I knew I had to look for my name and grab my own personal tray. I found it, but it was wrong. Erin A Brown, age 37 it read. It read the same as my hospital bracelet, which was also wrong. My middle initial is K, my age is 35. I thought of Elvis Aaron Presley when I picked it out of the pile for some reason, my mother's all-time favourite musician and thought of reincarnation, but I knew I wasn't Elvis in a past life. I couldn't be since he was still alive for a couple of months after I was born.

I sat down with my tray and ate my meal, listening to the conversation going on beside me between two patients. They were two females and one was looking through a magazine and picking out hairstyles that she liked. She was dressed in a hospital gown and overcoat.

I kept listening to their conversation while I ate. She began to speak of her boyfriend and how he beat her. It sounded as though she was trying to get away from him. Was she hiding here from him? But she was in a hospital gown. I finished my meal and got up to put my tray away. As I walked by the two girls I felt the need to say something. I don't know what I said now, but I allowed myself into their conversation for a brief moment, just an introduction. I felt a part of everything and everyone around me. We are all connected, even strangers, we are all human and alive and a part of this great and fascinating mystery of life. I put my tray away back on the tall silver tray rack.

I was given medication to help me sleep, Ativan I believe, and I was put back on my 10mgs of Cipralex. I believe the rest of the day and that evening I spent it mostly in my room and sleeping. Periodically a nurse would knock on my door and poke her nose in to see how I was doing. A few times I had my blood taken. I was finally getting some sleep.

I don't remember eating dinner. I do remember getting up a couple of times and helping myself to some juice and fruit in the communal fridge, a nurse told me I was allowed to do this. I would go right back to bed afterwards.

The next morning, I was awoken by a student nurse with an older nurse overseeing her. They wanted to take another blood sample; she was using a butterfly technique. I laid there and looked up at her, friendly and cooperatively. She seemed so young to me. She didn't make me feel odd even though I was a patient in this place, which I appreciated. She prepared my right arm while I lay in the bed. She pricked me with the little needle that had a butterfly shaped band on it and drew back my blood. I complimented her on a job well done and she grinned back at me and thanked me. The nurse that was accompanying her let me know that breakfast was ready whenever I am.

I lay in bed for a few moments longer before I decided to get up, still wearing the same clothes as yesterday and feeling no desire to change. I grabbed my toothbrush and went to the bathroom to brush my teeth. I still don't think the fact that I was in a psychiatric ward had completely sunk in, if at all. I never questioned it or thought much about it, I was simply going with the flow. No military thoughts. They had stayed in the bright room.

Breakfast was the same routine, look for your name on the tray on the rack. I sat down by myself and ate it. Others were eating around me. I saw that same girl who was in trouble with her boyfriend. I saw a young adult boy around his early twenties who seemed to be in a daze eating slowly. I would see him walking around with his eyes open and looking straight ahead without much expression at all, he was just moving.

When I was done with breakfast I put my tray away and went to the washroom to wash my hands and my face, then I started to head out to the double doors that were on the glass room side. There was still a nurse sitting there, reading while the same man was inside. He was curled up on the mattress under the covers sleeping.

"Long shift, eh," I said to the lady sitting at the little table reading. She looked exhausted. It was the same girl as last night. "I guess you'll be going home soon."

"Yes," she said. I could tell she was ready to go.

I walked through the double doors, smiling in at the nurses at their station as I did so. The television set was playing some country music videos. I sat down in one of the cushy chairs and tried to get comfortable. I got up and pulled another of the comfy chairs around so I would have something to put my feet up on, then I sat down again spreading my legs out and onto the seat of the chair I had just turned to face me. The nurses didn't seem to mind. While I watched the videos the girl I had seen earlier was attempting to play Ping-Pong with another patient, a male patient. She would play and talk and play a little more. She was revealing her life story to this boy; all about the boyfriend that beat her and tried to stab her. I was thinking about the music videos, glad to be watching them, dreaming about music.

Whenever anyone would walk by I would look at them. I would smile at the nurses. I would watch the patients. The boy that walks with no expression went by me a couple times. I cared about everyone here. I felt like we all just needed some help.

I grew tired of the television set. I looked around the room. The girl who was playing Ping-Pong was still lingering around, so I got up and asked her if she'd like to have a game with me. She was happy to oblige. So we walked over to the table together and each picked up a paddle. We hit the ball back and forth. I had more coordination than her. She seemed a little sluggish and distracted. I tried to get her to just focus on the ball. She liked to talk. We would hit the ball back and forth a couple times, and then she would miss and go to pick the ball up. She talked with me throughout most of our game. I listened to her and gave her advice the best that I could and I tried to take her mind off of her life outside these walls by focusing her on the game. I told her about the room with all the clothing and that she doesn't have to wear a hospital gown. She didn't know about this room. I guess not everyone knows about it, I thought. Maybe it was a special privilege of mine.

We were still playing when a nurse came over to me and told me I had a couple visitors. I excused myself from my game and went over to the door that led out to the hallway where I had originally come in. I wasn't allowed to leave yet. I had to wait.

Chapter Twenty – The Diagnosis

When I was given the go-ahead I opened the secure door and walked out to see Sarah and Christine waiting by the desk. I greeted them with a big toothy smile, although they looked very distraught and worried.

Christine looked very tired and run-down and as though she had been crying. There was a distant thought somewhere in the back of my mind that we were being kept separately in secure places safely away from Lane: We had to be kept in separate places so it would be more difficult for Lane to find us. At the forefront of my mind, however, I was elated to see the both of them, especially together. Sarah had met my one and only sister.

After our greeting of hugs and how are yous, we decided to go downstairs to the cafeteria to grab a drink together.

"Sure, you can go downstairs, Erin," the nurse behind the desk told me. "You just have to sign out right here. Write your name and the time you're leaving at. When you return, just sign in with the time you're back. Okay?"

"Okay, I got it," I smiled at her. Everyone seemed so helpful and kind.

I was still on a high. Again, I imagine if we all felt as elated as I did throughout this time it would be what it would be like to be in heaven. We would all have our individual personalities and gifts, yet we would be filled with love and wonder for everything around us and we would understand it all; the mystery would be revealed and the pain of human existence would be lifted from our hearts, minds and souls.

Going down the elevator I was ecstatic to tell Christine and Sarah about my new clothes, how much I really liked them and was going to take them with me when I leave.

We stepped out of the elevator and walked down the hallway towards the cafeteria. Sarah and my sister had already eaten prior to coming to visit with me; they had breakfast together and had discussed what had been going on with me.

I wandered through the cafeteria not really looking for anything; I had plenty of food to eat upstairs. Christine and I went to go and sit down while Sarah stayed back to grab us all a cup of hot coffee.

I was glad we were all together, my girlfriend, my sister and I all sitting together. Two of my favourite people in the world could get to know each other.

I talked about the people I met upstairs and the friends I'd made. I told them about the girl with the horrible boyfriend and how I listened to her and was trying to help her.

I asked about my brother Justin and his wife, and wondered how they were. I guess to me this was just an ordinary kind of visit. The severity of it had definitely not crossed my mind. Sarah told me that Justin and his wife would come out if they were needed. I thought that was nice of them.

"So, how's mom?" I asked Christine.

"She's good, she knows you're here." Again, my situation wasn't really sinking in. I was simply taking the information in stride.

Sarah told me how she was in transit most of the day before coming here. She had boarded a plane in Timmins early in the morning, had transferred in both Toronto and Calgary before finally arriving at her destination in Grande Prairie the night before around 11pm. She told me how she had taken a cab from the airport and booked into a hotel downtown. I was attempting to listen, but I was easily distracted with the amount of activity around me.

Over by the elevator I saw the young man from upstairs that walked with a slow float in his step and straight face. I told Christine and Sarah that I knew him and pointed over towards where he was standing and waiting. The elevator doors opened and he stepped inside.

"So what do you guys want to do now?" I asked cheerfully. I looked over behind me to see the sun shining through the windows. "It looks like a nice day outside, want to go for a walk?" I put my hands down on the table almost ready to get up and go as soon as I had asked.

Sarah and Christine both looked at each other a little hesitantly. "We can't. We have an appointment with your psychiatrist at 10am. We should be getting back," was Christine's response. Sarah agreed.

"Oh, okay then. She's really nice, you're going to like her," was my agreeable response.

We were all done with our coffees and so got up to dispose of them and carry on back to the elevator. Up we went to the 5th floor.

The elevator doors opened and I got off with a smiling face and greeted the nurse. I remembered to sign back in and jotted down the time of my return. They opened the doors for us. A nurse led us to a little room a little further down on the right side with the writing "Visitors Room" on the door. There were chairs to sit down on, a little coffee table with magazines on it. We chose our seats and waited with each other.

I was just so happy to have my girls together. I bragged to Christine about how cute Sarah is. "Isn't she gorgeous?" I said, maybe embarrassing both of them. I got up and gave Sarah a big kiss on the mouth and hugged her. I had the best girl. I was proud of both my girls sitting here with me.

"You guys want to see my room?"

"We're not allowed to leave this room," Sarah told me.

"What?"

"That's what the nurses told us, we have to stay here."

It's situations like this where I don't like authority. I can see now why the rules would be to keep the visitors away from the rest of the patients; it is respect for their privacy and well-being. At the time, however, I felt like breaking the rules and going against the binds of authority. In reality I was only thinking of myself and what I wanted at the moment.

"We could have a game of Ping-Pong," I suggested.

"Erin, they don't want us out there."

Christine left to use the washroom. Sarah and I remained in the little visitor's room with four walls around us and nothing to do.

"Come on, it'll be okay," I said without thinking anything of it. I got up and led Sarah out of the room. We walked across the lounge area over to the big windows on the other side. Sarah was walking cautiously. I was happy I was getting what I wanted.

"Look at this view," I motioned to her. She stepped up beside me and looked out.

It wasn't long before a nurse came over to us. She was firm with me. "Erin, you have to stay in the visitor's area or your guests will have to leave."

I didn't argue. I could sense she was getting angry and I didn't want any trouble. We walked back to the little room and sat back down.

"What's the big deal?" I was disappointed. "I just wanted to play a game of Ping-Pong. There's nothing for us to do here. If someone comes to visit and all they can do is sit in this little room…"

"Then they'll just leave," Sarah finished my sentence for me. She knew what I was talking about. I was a little frustrated.

Outside the door I could see the girl in the hospital gown walking slowly over to the pay phone hanging on the wall across the room.

"You're not like that," Sarah said to me. I looked at her and thought of course I'm not. Then I realized she said it to me because I was also a patient in this place.

Christine rejoined us. We sat together a little while longer when a nurse came to let me know I had a phone call. She informed me that I could use the phone that was hanging on the wall just outside of this room to the right of the doorway.

The phone was just a grey box hanging on the wall. I picked up the receiver. "Hello?"

"Erin? How are you?"

"Justin?" It was my brother. It meant a lot to me that Justin was calling. I felt bonded to him because he knew what it was like to be in a place like this. I told him I was fine, that Christine and Sarah were here with me. He made sure that I knew getting rest was the most important thing for me right now. We didn't talk long, just enough so that I knew he was thinking of me and that he cared.

Shortly after that the psychiatrist arrived. She introduced herself to Sarah and Christine before she sat down to join us. She began by asking me a few routine questions and then wanted to speak with Sarah and Christine alone. They left the room together. I stayed and waited.

While they were gone a young slightly overweight Asian girl came into the room and pulled up a chair in front of me. She handed me a two-page purple copy of some kind of questionnaire. I couldn't figure out if this was some kind of person in training or if they were another patient simply thinking they were in training. I looked at the questionnaire. On the top left hand side there was a box that read Alberta Health Services 5 South-Inpatient Psychiatric Admission Assessment Social History-Patient Portion. It had a sticker beside this box with my name, age, date of birth and some number and letter coding. Again, my age, name and date of birth were not entirely correct. This felt surreal to me. While she was talking to me and telling me that if I wanted to fill out this questionnaire it was completely voluntary I kept wondering who she was. She looked to me like a young version of the first psychiatrist I had seen while I was still downstairs in the holding room. It felt as though this was that person at a younger age trying to work herself up in the ranks of psychiatric work. Time was strange for me, almost eternal and past and present didn't add up in my thoughts. Neither did the fact that they were opposite sexes. I felt as though we lived many lifetimes and I was given a glimpse of someone else's incarnations. She informed me that if I wanted to skip any questions that that was okay as well. I was polite, and listened to her as she spoke, holding the questionnaire in my hands. She gave me a pen.

When she left I looked over the questionnaire.

This questionnaire will assist the treatment team with your care plan. The questions are not mandatory. Any questions you feel uncomfortable with may be discussed with your nurse/doctor, or left blank. **PLEASE COMPLETE IN INK**

There were two full pages, both double sided, with questions. I never answered one of them.

Meanwhile, the psychiatrist informed Christine and Sarah that she had had a chance to speak with me and she knows what is going on. She told them that I was diagnosed as being Bi-Polar. Since Sarah was living with me she wanted to know more about my behaviour previous to this event, if how I was acting at this time is a reflection of my normal behaviour. Sarah let her know that I wasn't normally this happy. She told the psychiatrist about the stressors in my life at the time and that I was often depressed.

They were both informed that I had experienced a psychosis and was now coming down in a manic state. I needed a lot of rest and relaxation. She would allow me to leave with Sarah because she trusted Sarah with me; otherwise she would normally keep me in the hospital for a couple more days. Again, she stressed to them how important it was for me to get lots of rest.

When they came back into the room I was informed that I could be released. "I'm letting you go," the Psychiatrist said. "But I'm only letting you go because I trust that Sarah can look after you, otherwise I would keep you here longer, do you understand?"

"Yes," I said.

"You need to get lots of rest."

I was informed by the psychiatrist about the medication I would be prescribed. I was to keep taking my 10mgs of Cipralex in the morning and was to also take 25 mgs of Seroquil at night before I go to bed. I let the doctor know that I did not have a drug plan at this time; because of this she said she would prescribe me 25 mg of Chlorpromazine rather than Seroquel. She said it was an older drug that is still effective but a lot less expensive.

"Will I become immune to the medication and have to be prescribed a higher dosage at some time?"

"No, it doesn't work that way."

"What about my creativity? I like to write and play the guitar. Will the medication take that away from me?"

"No, you will be the same person." She was very direct with her responses, like she has answered these questions many times before and was tired of them.

"Now," the psychiatrist looked at me, "what do you think is happening?" She continued to stare at me.

I looked right back at her and said, "Sarah is taking me home." Of course, I was chipper and happy about it and gave the psychiatrist my trademark big smile.

The Doctor said she would give me some extra medication that was in this facility to keep me until I can get back to my nurse practitioner and have my subscriptions filled. She left the room and returned with a handful of boxes of Seroquel. I already had enough of my own Cipralex to do me.

"Do you have any other questions?" Our meeting was coming to an end.

"Yes," I said. "Are YOU on any medication?"

She looked at me, and in a calm voice said "No." With a straight face she stood up. I stood up as well and motioned to offer her a hug. She looked at me, hesitated for a fraction of a second and walked forward to allow me to hug her goodbye. I thanked her and watched her walk slowly out the door.

I was free to go. I was officially high-tailing it out of this joint!

Chapter Twenty-One – A Long Journey Home

As soon as the Doctor had left the room, I turned to my girls and said, "I'll go get my stuff and meet you guys outside the doors."

My head was held high and I was walking with great posture heading towards my room. I was granted a great honour, my freedom.

As I got closer to the door of my room I saw an old man sitting in a wheelchair just beside it. He looked so sad to me. "Hello, sir," I greeted him as I approached. He looked at me, slowly moving his head towards my direction. "Are you okay?"

He told me how he wanted to be transferred to the Hythe Continuing Care Centre, an old age home not far from Beaverlodge. I still had the questionnaire and pen in my hand, so I asked him his name and wrote down on the top of the first page, 'Don Quinn wants to go to the Hythe Continuing Care'. I told him I lived in Beaverlodge for several years and I know Hythe well. He looked like he was happy to hear that.

I went into my room and started to put my belongings in a plastic bag. I opened the dresser doors and put my few articles of clothing in the bag, as well as a tattoo magazine that I had become attached to and my toothpaste and toothbrush. I already had the playing cards in my pocket and I added the toy truck, the motorcycle lighter and the beaver beer cap to my pocket collection as well. I had everything.

When I was leaving my room, I turned to Don Quinn while putting my hand in my pocket feeling for the beaver cap and pulled it out of my pocket. "See, this is my symbol for Beaverlodge," I said to him happily. He looked at it and nodded his head with a smile. "Goodbye Don."

"Good bye."

Back in the common room I saw the girl with the boyfriend troubles. I walked over to her and said, "I'm getting out of here!"

"Really?" She seemed impressed and surprised at the same time.

"Yeah!" I beamed at her. "Listen, you take care of yourself, you hear?"

She smiled at me, "I will."

I walked over to the secure door. Four workers were standing there. One of the nurses gave me back my wallet and cell phone. "Thank you for all of your help," I said to them. They were smiling at me and wishing me well. I gave them all a hug goodbye.

Outside the doors, Christine and Sarah were waiting for me.

We went to lunch at a joint nearby where I talked the waitress up and was my usual manic over-confident self. I talked throughout the whole meal to Sarah and Christine, taking control of the conversation in a chipper and excited tone.

The thoughts I had throughout my psychotic state were no longer there. I knew where I was, I knew I was going back home with Sarah, but still the significance of what I had gone through and the meaning of my diagnosis escaped me. At this moment I was simply excitable and resembling a child who has ADHD.

After lunch Christine drove Sarah and I over to our hotel before saying our farewells. She needed to get back to her family and she and Sarah believed I needed to get to the hotel to rest. I was finally okay with Christine going home. I didn't feel as though she was in danger. A part of me was beginning to realize what I had done at her home, but my mind wasn't fully ready to register it all. I just felt like I shouldn't go there just yet.

We took my duffel bags, violin and knapsack out of her car and placed them on the pavement for now. We hugged each other goodbye, not knowing when we'd see each other again for a while and off she went.

Sarah and I went to Giant Tiger to pick out a bathing suit for me. I wouldn't normally let her pick it out herself, but I was simply along for the ride at this point. We didn't take long to get a black bikini in my size and I was feeling bold enough to wear it even though all my other bathing suits have only been one piece.

Back at the hotel, Sarah showed me to the room we'd be staying in for the night and we decided to go for a swim and a hot tub right away. We got changed into our bikinis, wrapped our towels around our wastes and put a t-shirt on over top for the walk down the long hallway.

Walking into the pool area I was enveloped by the warm steamy air, the kind of warmth that wraps itself around you and invites you to stay awhile. The pool area was completely empty, except for us. I walked over to the white plastic chairs that were sitting near the hot tub and took my t-shirt and towel off and placed them on one of the chairs.

I stepped into the hot tub slowly taking one step at a time and feeling the heat of the water beginning to surround me. I sat down at the far end and let out a sigh of comfort and relaxation. Sarah joined me.

After a little time had passed I got out to swim some laps. Sarah stayed in the hot tub while I breast-stroked back and forth across the pool. When I'd had enough I went and joined her in the warmth again.

~

When we got back to the room I took a shower right away. When I was finished and changed I went out to the bedroom area and found Sarah had turned on the television set and was waiting for her turn to take a shower. I continued to get dressed and towel off my hair while she was washing off. Then I sat down at the head of one of the beds and looked for something to watch on T.V. Nothing was really catching my interest and by the time Sarah was done in the shower I was ready to do something else. Afterall, here we were in Grande Prairie, a place I had lived near and known for almost seven years. I wanted to show Sarah around a little bit; I wanted to take her to places I had loved while living here.

We were both dressed and refreshed, why not hit the town? "I know of this really cool bookstore downtown, not too far away, we could walk there easily from here. It's called The Rabbit Hole. We should go and check it out, I'd love to show it to you," I suggested.

"No, Erin, we should just stay here and relax."

"But it's not very far and there's a couple other cool little stores that I know you'll love."

"No, it's better if we just stay here. We can go for another hot tub a little later and you can go for another swim." Sarah was firm in her response.

I was getting a little frustrated. I didn't understand why she would want to spend her whole time in this hotel room when I wanted to show her a couple places that I had loved while I lived out here.

"Come on, Sarah, when are we ever going to be back here? It could be years for all we know. I just want to show you this bookstore, I know you'll love it!"

Sarah was still firmly against it and I could sense that she wasn't going to budge in her opinion. I was feeling caged in and frustrated that Sarah wouldn't just come with me. I knew however, that there was nothing I could say to change her mind. I was very disappointed. My emotional reactions were easily triggered. I was getting upset and feeling like I was being controlled. Sarah was frustrated and feeling like I was getting out of control.

I started to think about calling Fen. Here I was in Grande Prairie and I wanted to see how my old best friend was doing. Maybe I could have a quick visit with her before I head back to Ontario. There was a lot I wanted to do before getting on that plane tomorrow. I had had a whole life in this neck of the woods, and here I was stuck in a hotel room not allowed to go anywhere.

Sarah argued with me about calling Fen. In her mind I wasn't fit to do anything, which she was right. But in my mind, I was capable of doing whatever I wanted to do and I didn't appreciate being told I wasn't. I looked up the number to Fen's bakery and tried calling it on my cell phone. No answer.

Sarah and I fought some more. I think we had gotten so used to fighting with each other that it just seemed like normal conversation. My emotions got the best of me; they were easily triggered and erupted at the struggle between us. I wanted to explore, Sarah wanted to stay confined to one room.

We had a blowout.

I left in a huff by myself. I was going to walk over to Fen's bakery and visit her whether Sarah liked it or not. I didn't want to be told what I could and couldn't do.

I got outside and started walking down one of the main roads that would take me to the other end of the city. I was walking with fervor at a quickened pace. My mind was full of emotion, anger, frustration. My body was charged up. After five to ten minutes I began to cool down and slow my pace. I wanted to be calm. I took deep breaths and walked at a more leisurely pace. I wanted to be at one with myself, I didn't want my emotions to get the best of me.

As I continued walking I began to realize just how far it would be to walk all the way over to Fen's bakery. It was ridiculously far, and then what, I'd have to walk back. I didn't even know if she was going to be there. I hadn't really thought this through.

I turned around and started heading back towards the hotel.

When I get back to the room, Sarah tells me she is going to get another room for herself. She's had enough, she says.

"You're just going to leave me?"

"I can't handle anymore," she says.

She can't handle anymore? What about me? All I wanted to do was take her to look at a GODDAMN bookstore! I wanted to show her a part of my past and it ended up being a federal FUCKING case! That's how I was feeling. Poor Sarah was only trying to follow the Doctor's orders.

Even though Sarah and I were fighting, I didn't want to be left alone. I didn't want her to go. We talked more calmly with each other and tried to work through the argument. Sarah was trying to explain to me that she was under strict orders to make sure I get lots of rest and relaxation. I listened to her, not really thinking going to a bookstore was an exuberant use of energy, but I didn't want to fight anymore either. So I agreed to stay in the hotel and try to simply relax.

For the rest of the day, we stayed lying down and vegging out to the television set. We only left the room to get some dinner at one of the restaurants downstairs in the lobby of our hotel. I had been to this restaurant before. This whole city was filled with memories for me. Now, I was a ghost in this town.

After we finished our meal we went back upstairs to our room. We stayed there for the rest of the night. I took my medication and at some point fell asleep.

The next morning we packed our stuff up and went to check out of the hotel. The clerk at the desk allowed us to keep our bags behind the counter while we went in to have breakfast at the Denny's that was attached to the hotel.

At breakfast Sarah was still tense. I was trying to be light and easy. Our conversation was forced. Sarah was mostly quiet. Our meal was spent mostly listening to each other chew. This agitated me a little bit and I wanted to do something that would spice up our time. So I reached over for my violin and took it out of its case.

Sarah was trying to stop me the whole time, "Erin, what are you doing, don't, put that away." But I continued to have a little fun. I put the violin up to my chin and started to make a little noise on it. People were starting to look over at us.

I didn't play long, just a quick little moment of surprise. I saw some of the other customers smiling my way. I didn't think anyone cared, except maybe Sarah. She was embarrassed and mad at me for making a scene. I felt like I was just being fun and carefree. I put the violin back in its case, still glowing from having played it. I just thought if I was a patron in that situation and some stranger did that around me I would be amused, even if they didn't know how to play. Sure, maybe some people would make fun of me, but who cares? It's something that doesn't happen every day, but Sarah didn't see it that way. She thought I was just making a scene and she found the fact that I was drawing attention to us extremely uncomfortable and embarrassing. For once I just wanted her to be carefree with me.

We finished our meal and paid the bill, called a taxi, grabbed our bags and waited outside the lobby doors for it to arrive.

The cabbie showed up and immediately helped us to put our bags in the trunk. We both got in the backseat.

"Where to?"

"The airport," Sarah replied.

Most of the ride was silent. I looked out the window quietly saying goodbye to the old familiar scenery around me, not knowing when I would see it again. I said goodbye to the big and vast Alberta sky.

We had an hour to kill at the airport so we spent it outside lying in the sun on a patch of grass next to a tree. I was still a little hyper, but Sarah was quiet and withdrawn. She had removed her outer sweater and had laid it down on the grass underneath her so it could be between her and the blades of grass. She had her dark sunglasses on and her one arm draped across her forehead.

It was a long and quiet flight home.

Chapter Twenty-Two – Recovery

"Know Thyself" - Socrates

It wasn't until I had gotten home and back into our apartment that the exhaustion of the past week and a half had finally completely overcome my mind and body. For the next three days I would sleep off and on throughout the day, as well as sleep soundly through the night. Sarah and I took her dog for a walk around the park trail at one time, but I didn't have the strength to keep up with them. I had to sit down on a bench and wait. This is when I began to fully realize just how much I had gone through.

Different family members were calling me to see how I was, my mother, my father, my grandparents, my brothers. When Christine called me we talked about some of the things that I had said and done while in the psychosis. I was laughing at some of the ridiculousness of it and taking most of it in stride while at the same time being in shock at all that had happened. But the worst was over now. My psychosis had completely passed.

I had made an appointment to get my prescriptions filled at the Medical Clinic in Kirkland Lake, Ontario. Doctors from down south are rotated through their clinic on a regular basis. This particular Doctor of the week that I had seen thought I should book an appointment to see a psychiatrist for a check-up and to talk about what had happened. I agreed. She said it would probably take up to three months before I could see someone and that the clinic would call me to let me know when the next available appointment would be. I never received a phone call. I never did talk to any professionals about what had happened. I decided that I didn't need to and that I could handle it on my own.

I'm only fully coming to grips with being diagnosed as being Bi-Polar now, a year after my psychosis and diagnosis. Before now it just seemed like an obscure title to me, something that held no real significance. But I've since had a chance to really think about my life and how my behaviour has been in the past, especially my emotional behaviour. Now, I feel a lot healthier and happier than ever before because I'm much more stable in my emotions and thoughts. I'm thankful for my medication. I know it is giving me a higher quality of life, although I still don't like going to the drugstore to pick them up. I also sleep a lot more soundly now and even remember many of my dreams. Remembering my dreams is something that I've been lacking for almost ten years.

It might sound strange to some, but I am grateful for having gone through my psychosis. Without having reached this state of mind, I might never have been diagnosed. Without that diagnosis I wouldn't have been on the proper medication. Without the proper medication I wouldn't be as stable as I am now. So, I'm glad it happened. Now all my cards are laid out on the table and I can deal with a full deck. The game isn't rigged for me anymore. It is much better to go through life knowing and understanding yourself and staring it in the face than to be in the dark. That way you can accept yourself and live a fuller life.

underneath her so it could be between her and the blades of grass. She had her dark sunglasses on and her one arm draped across her forehead.

It was a long and quiet flight home.

Chapter Twenty-Two – Recovery

"Know Thyself" - Socrates

It wasn't until I had gotten home and back into our apartment that the exhaustion of the past week and a half had finally completely overcome my mind and body. For the next three days I would sleep off and on throughout the day, as well as sleep soundly through the night. Sarah and I took her dog for a walk around the park trail at one time, but I didn't have the strength to keep up with them. I had to sit down on a bench and wait. This is when I began to fully realize just how much I had gone through.

Different family members were calling me to see how I was, my mother, my father, my grandparents, my brothers. When Christine called me we talked about some of the things that I had said and done while in the psychosis. I was laughing at some of the ridiculousness of it and taking most of it in stride while at the same time being in shock at all that had happened. But the worst was over now. My psychosis had completely passed.

I had made an appointment to get my prescriptions filled at the Medical Clinic in Kirkland Lake, Ontario. Doctors from down south are rotated through their clinic on a regular basis. This particular Doctor of the week that I had seen thought I should book an appointment to see a psychiatrist for a check-up and to talk about what had happened. I agreed. She said it would probably take up to three months before I could see someone and that the clinic would call me to let me know when the next available appointment would be. I never received a phone call. I never did talk to any professionals about what had happened. I decided that I didn't need to and that I could handle it on my own.

I'm only fully coming to grips with being diagnosed as being Bi-Polar now, a year after my psychosis and diagnosis. Before now it just seemed like an obscure title to me, something that held no real significance. But I've since had a chance to really think about my life and how my behaviour has been in the past, especially my emotional behaviour. Now, I feel a lot healthier and happier than ever before because I'm much more stable in my emotions and thoughts. I'm thankful for my medication. I know it is giving me a higher quality of life, although I still don't like going to the drugstore to pick them up. I also sleep a lot more soundly now and even remember many of my dreams. Remembering my dreams is something that I've been lacking for almost ten years.

It might sound strange to some, but I am grateful for having gone through my psychosis. Without having reached this state of mind, I might never have been diagnosed. Without that diagnosis I wouldn't have been on the proper medication. Without the proper medication I wouldn't be as stable as I am now. So, I'm glad it happened. Now all my cards are laid out on the table and I can deal with a full deck. The game isn't rigged for me anymore. It is much better to go through life knowing and understanding yourself and staring it in the face than to be in the dark. That way you can accept yourself and live a fuller life.